HANOI STORIES

In memory of my father
William James Hunt, 1917–2003

HANOI STORIES

Eight wonderful years in Vietnam's capital

PAM SCOTT

First published in Australia in 2004 by
New Holland Publishers (Australia) Pty Ltd
Sydney • Auckland • London • Cape Town

14 Aquatic Drive Frenchs Forest NSW 2086 Australia
218 Lake Road Northcote Auckland New Zealand
86 Edgware Road London W2 2EA United Kingdom
80 McKenzie Street Cape Town 8001 South Africa

National Library of Australia Cataloguing-in-Publication Data:

Scott, Pam
Hanoi stories: eight wonderful years in Vietnam's capital

ISBN 1 74110 097 6

1. Scott, Pam. 2. Australians—Vietnam—Hanoi. 3. Bookstores
Vietnam—Hanoi. 4. Hanoi (Vietnam)—Description and travel. I. Title.

915.7

Publishing Manager: Robynne Millward
Copy Editor: Karen Gee
Designer: Joanne Buckley
Production Controller: Kellie Matterson
Printer: McPherson's Printing Group

10 9 8 7 6 5 4 3 2

FOREWORD

Australia was one of the first Western countries to open an embassy in Hanoi, in 1973, shortly after withdrawing from the war we called the Vietnam War, and the Vietnamese called the American War. When Vietnam began to open up in the late 1980s, Australian companies were among the first to come in. One of the earliest, and most successful, was the Australian telecommunications company Telstra, which persuaded the Vietnamese that the key to a modern economy was international telecommunications, and that these could not only be self-funding, but could produce revenue for a government facing increasing demands for services by its people. Pam Scott came to Vietnam with a Telstra training program for the Vietnamese company VNPT.

When I arrived as Australian Ambassador in Hanoi in 1994, the United States was still refusing to recognise the communist state and Australia was Vietnam's most influential foreign partner, providing recognition and international access to a state desperate to modernise (but on its own terms) and to take its place in the world.

Pam Scott was one of the first Australians I met in Hanoi. She was a striking, beautifully groomed 'older' woman, living 'local' and alone in the Vietnam Post and Telegraph Company guesthouse, and riding around the countryside fearlessly with a range of Vietnamese friends, on the backs of motorbikes. She had left behind family, comfort and security in Australia and decided to throw herself wholeheartedly into a new and challenging country. She was hugely successful and, while always pleased to be included in embassy events and to share her friendship and experiences with the somewhat eccentric Australian Ambassador, did not look to us for shelter or entertainment. She was too busy living her new life to the full—as this book reveals.

Australians were appreciated in Vietnam: we had a similar sense of humour to the Vietnamese, we were not 'up ourselves', we did not stand on dignity, we were prepared to roll up our sleeves and get on with the job, we were honest, egalitarian, friendly, and provided a much desired avenue to the outside world, to commerce, to education, to Western culture, to international recognition.

And Australians, like Pam, were in turn enraptured by Vietnam—by the physical beauty of the country and its people, by the strength and power of its culture, by the resilience of its people, by the importance attached to personal relationships, and the capacity of a people to enjoy and live their lives on a very weak material base. And no matter how much we tried to give, we all gained so much more!

Vietnam remains my favourite posting, in a long foreign service career. It gets under your skin—and I suspect neither Pam nor I have closed off the Vietnam chapter of our lives.

Pam has documented superbly and personally the small details that illuminate life in Vietnam in the 1990s. Her book is a great read.

Susan (Sue) Boyd
Australian Ambassador in Vietnam 1994–1998

CONTENTS

I want to straddle big winds, to tread on ferocious waves, to behead the ocean's sharks, to chase away aggressors...I cannot resign myself to bowing down and becoming a man's concubine.

Trieu Thi Trinh
Vietnamese female leader of an uprising against the Chinese,
3rd century AD

ACKNOWLEDGMENTS

I owe an enormous debt of gratitude to the Vietnamese people who befriended and helped me in so many ways, and ultimately gave me the stories recorded here. Some are identified by name, but in other cases I have changed their identity to protect them from any unwanted attention. Thanks also to those expatriates living in Hanoi who shared some of my adventures and provided a sympathetic ear when things went wrong, especially Shuna Akerman, Andrea Flew and Vilaisan Campbell; all my bookshop customers, especially Hugh and Deborah, whose visits always resulted in record sales; the terrific group of women who came and went over the years and inspired me; and Sue Boyd who brought humour and a woman's touch to the embassy during her term as Australian Ambassador in Vietnam, and who graciously agreed to write a foreword to this book.

There are moments in life when we are nudged along a new path. Thanks to Ian Reinecke, Peter Davies, Suzanne Hosley and Dick Harman for opening unexpected doors for me. To Robynne Millward, publishing manager at New Holland, who responded so positively to my manuscript, and Karen Gee, my gentle, skilful editor who whipped it into shape...many thanks for making my transition to author almost too easy. To all of them I am grateful for the belief they had in me and for the opportunities they provided.

Thanks also to my friends Diana van Oort and Mr Cuong for their photos, and David Curtin for his criticism and encouragement.

Vietnamese fortune tellers would regularly tell me that Vietnam was part of my destiny and would be good for me. Perhaps they were right. I (and my family and friends) thought

I had taken an irrational leap into the unknown when I first went to live in Vietnam, but Hanoi, with all its charms, was there to catch me and hold on to me. I received so much more from the adventure than I can ever hope to repay.

PROLOGUE
My love affair with Hanoi

Is it possible to fall in love with a city? I wouldn't have thought so once—but that was before I had been to Hanoi. I suppose I love my home city of Sydney, but that is more like the way you love your parents. It's where you come from, it's always there, and you don't usually have to think about it. Hanoi was more like a passionate affair.

I knew I was captured after three short visits in 1993, and it was an emotional parting on what I thought would be my last trip. The trade mission was over, and the training program I had been involved in was also finished, so there was no reason for me to return. There were sad partings from new friends who sang me haunting traditional songs of farewell, a last *cyclo* ride around the city, armfuls of flowers to colour and perfume my departure, and then tears all the way from Hanoi to Singapore.

Why did I feel this way? Until my first visit, I had no particular interest in Vietnam or even any knowledge of the country, apart from the images of war which for years had thrust their way into our homes via television and newspapers and, later, the images of 'boat people' and the xenophobic rantings they inspired. I was born in Australia in 1945, the same year Vietnamese leader Ho Chi Minh made his declaration of independence and pronounced the Democratic Republic of Vietnam. But 1945 was a pretty historic year, so that particular fact about a small Asian nation escaped my notice. My brother was born in the year the French were defeated at Dien Bien Phu, but I didn't make this connection until recently. I was busy graduating from Sydney University during the Kennedy administration and the Tonkin Gulf incident, worrying about my first job when the first US combat troops landed at Da Nang, and busy setting up house as a new bride as the war escalated. My sons were born in 1970 and 1972 during those years of fighting and tragic loss of lives. And I was submerged in a private world far removed from those horrors, doing small battle with sleepless nights, nappy rash and feeding problems. When I could finally look up from the daily grind of babies and housework, I found that the South had been 'liberated' and the age of innocence for the West was over.

For the next decade, Vietnam and I closed our doors on the world. I was busy gaining three more university degrees, surviving a divorce, and caring for my children. When we opened our doors to the world again in 1986, I had a PhD and Vietnam had a new Secretary General of the Communist Party and a new 'open door' policy of *doi moi*, or economic reform.

Later, Vietnamese fortune tellers would tell me that Vietnam was my destiny and that I should stay there for a long time since it was 'like a fairyland' for me. And that seemed to be the case. Not long after returning to Australia from my last visit at the end of 1993 I was offered a job in Hanoi—initially for six months, then another six months and another. When one job ended, another would appear. First I worked for three years as a consultant in the telecommunications industry, providing advice to Vietnam Post and Telecom and to multinationals wanting to do business with them. Then I worked on a Swedish government-funded capacity-building project to develop a business school at the National Economics University in Hanoi for two years, where I taught on international MBA programs. When that project ended, I moved to CARE International, where I managed a large UN-funded capacity-building project for two years. After that I started a small human resources management consultancy with a Vietnamese friend who had been one of my MBA students, and I also decided to open a much-needed English language bookshop with Minh, another Vietnamese friend.

Eight years passed. It seemed as though I had lived in Hanoi forever, but at the same time it seemed like just the briefest of times and I couldn't imagine leaving. And then suddenly, in early 2002, it felt time to go home. But I would never be the same after this completely unexpected adventure, where I discovered as much about myself and my society as I did about the Vietnamese and their society. What I found in no way matched those stark stereotypes of Vietcong and boat people that I had in my head. Where I expected to find bitterness and resentment, I found none; no grievances about the past, only hope for the future. Where I expected to feel the repressiveness of a communist state, I felt safe, free and unrestricted. Where I expected coldness towards the West, I found warmth and friendship, curiosity and openness. Where I expected that poverty and hardship would have lowered spirits and aspirations, I found fun and laughter, singing and dancing, support for and interest in the arts, and a surprisingly literate and intellectual society. And where I expected to find the East, I found an intriguing blend of East and West, mixed together in a uniquely Vietnamese way—like a Vietnamese spring roll, which takes various fruits and vegetables and meat, wraps them in rice paper and dips them in a specially blended sauce. Vietnam has its basis in Chinese tradition and this forms the rice paper wrapping for bits and pieces of culture from France, the former Soviet Union, the United States, and neighbouring Indochinese countries. But it is the unique Vietnamese sauce that provides that special, tantalising flavour.

My work brought me into contact with a wide range of people involved in government, business, aid and academia, at all levels. My 'play' increased my range of friendships and my exposure to all aspects of Vietnamese life. I travelled to all parts of the country, celebrated national holidays, visited pagodas, joined weddings and funerals, met the extended families of my friends and went to their home villages. I learned to sing Vietnamese songs with a famous Vietnamese singer, had ballroom dancing lessons, drumming lessons, table tennis lessons, Vietnamese language lessons. I got to know my neighbours, local shopkeepers, dressmakers, hairdressers, pedicurists, waiters, shoeshine boys and postcard sellers, post office workers, bread sellers, dancers, singers, teachers, doctors, fortune tellers, Party officials, police, government ministers, company directors, noodle sellers. I learnt and experienced so much through them as they generously took me into their worlds.

Being alone in a strange country, away from the responsibilities of family, free from social obligations and with none of the distractions of everyday life, like films and television, can be a wonderful opportunity to immerse yourself in your adopted culture. The Vietnamese proved to be extremely willing partners in this exercise, taking me under their wing and into their lives. They love to play, they love to show you their history and culture, and they are enormously curious about everything. The stories that follow are sketches of some of my experiences during the eight wonderful years I spent in Hanoi. They are funny, sad, sometimes inspirational: in some I have tried to document a way of life fast disappearing, or show the trials and tribulations of living and working in Hanoi for both locals and expatriates; but most of all I have tried to introduce you to some of the friends I made and through them show what everyday life was like in a city going through a period of enormous political, economic and social change in the last decade of the 20th century.

Living at the Post Office Guesthouse

I will never forget my first impression of what was to be my new home in Hanoi. My family and friends thought I was slightly crazy, suddenly leaving a comfortable life to go and work in Hanoi, and as the minibus from the airport brought me closer and closer to the Post Office Guesthouse in Tran Quoc Toan Street, I was beginning to think they might be right.

Flying into Hanoi's Noi Bai airport on a clear day can afford some wonderful views: spread out below, a patchwork of rice fields wrapped in ribbons of water; in the distance, mountains and unexpected areas of forest. As you descend, you get a bird's-eye view of palm tree-shaded collections of bamboo and mud-brick homes, forming a network of communities joined by a crisscross of narrow dirt roads. Occasionally you might spy a town with more substantial buildings, and maybe a pagoda or cemetery. Soothed by the airline landing muzak, the scene below seems peaceful and timeless, a picture of rural life long gone from our modern cities. But after labouring through customs and immigration procedures, you finally burst forth from your comfortable temporary womb and find yourself gulping for breath in an all-too-real world where all your senses are assaulted simultaneously.

These days there is a modern highway between Hanoi and the airport, busy with airport buses and taxis, and the trip takes just a little over half an hour. But back in 1994, the trip to town took an hour or more and the transport was more than likely an ancient Russian-made rust bucket that had to be nursed and cajoled by its driver as it limped to its destination. Sharing the road with you were buffalo or ponies pulling carts or being led by old ladies or small children; trucks large and small, but all dirty, dilapidated and belching smoke; local buses over-laden with people, livestock, bicycles, boxes and baskets; *cyclos* carrying people, machinery, furniture or animals; maybe a flock of geese or ducks being herded along; a few dogs sleeping in the middle of the road; and vast numbers of bicycles and motorbikes, all seemingly performing death-defying stunts. Along the side of the road there were crowds of people going about their business, carrying things, selling things, repairing or building things, eating, drinking, working in the fields, loading and unloading, or just standing or sitting, watching the world go by. And it all seemed to be happening without any system, any rules or logic, and to the sound of loud and constant honking of horns. Ask foreigners living in Hanoi which side of the road Vietnamese drive on and they'll tell you, 'your side, and usually coming straight at you!' But if you can manage to relax enough to ignore the immediate mayhem and look further afield, you will recapture some of the enchantment you saw earlier from the air. As far as the eye can see, rice field upon rice field, conical hats bobbing among the green stalks, women old and young carrying water, planting, digging, reaping, following timeless patterns. When the sun casts a certain glow, it is easy to think you have been dropped into a movie set with only the epic soundtrack missing.

I had negotiated a seat in a minibus with some other travellers and given the driver the address I wanted. As we drove further into the centre of Hanoi, the streets became even more crowded and chaotic. As the driver prepared to pull up I remember looking pityingly at my fellow passengers, wondering who was the unfortunate one who would be staying in this slum area of derelict buildings, piles of rubbish, people washing at a public tap, others sitting by the road selling meat and fish, fruit and vegetables. And then the driver pointed at me! This was going to be my new neighbourhood, and suddenly I wasn't sure I was going to make it.

On my earlier short visits to Vietnam I had made some friends in high places, and they had arranged permission for me to rent a room in the Post Office Guesthouse in Hanoi. Accommodation for foreigners was not easy to find in Hanoi at that time. There were a few hotels for short-term stays, but as the number of foreigners coming to stay for business increased, suitable housing was at a premium. Vietnamese who owned property were busy building and renovating and obtaining government permission to rent to foreigners, and the rewards were huge. It was not uncommon at the height of the investment boom in Vietnam for foreign company directors to pay US$8000 to US$10 000 per month for a large house on West Lake. Often a year's rent in advance was required, allowing the owner to immediately start work building another house, and many Hanoi fortunes were made this way. The Asian economic downturn in 1997 and an eventual oversupply led to sharply falling rentals, but in 1994 my US$660 per month rental for a rather spartan room in the Post Office Guesthouse was considered very reasonable.

This four-storey guesthouse building attached to the head-quarters of Vietnam Post and Telecom (VNPT) was mainly used by staff from the provinces when they came to Hanoi on business. The director-general also had a room there, dividing his time between Hanoi and his home in Ho Chi Minh City. I was given the room next to his, and when he retired some eighteen months later, I was upgraded and allowed to have his old room since the new director-general already had a home in Hanoi. Despite my initial misgivings, it turned out to be a most fortuitous decision to stay there. Working as a consultant for VNPT, providing strategic advice to foreign companies hoping to do business with the state-owned company, I was ideally situated as I had access to all the 'right' people and information, and had the opportunity to build good relationships with VNPT staff. Just as importantly, I was well looked after by the guesthouse staff and felt part of a large extended family.

But as well as that, Hanoi soon worked its special magic and very quickly I was seeing with different eyes. What began as a blur of sensory overload soon became a series of fascinating vignettes—sad, funny, poignant, mystifying, inspiring. The signs of poverty, the dirt and disorder all faded, and now I only saw the vibrancy and colour, the energy, beauty and optimism in the life of my street. There was the barber opposite, who always looked immaculately groomed, with his barber's chair set up on the pavement under the shade of a tree and a mirror hung on the wall. Nearby was the motorbike-washing business where customers sat on a long stool on the pavement opposite to avoid getting splashed while their motorbike was hand-washed. Then there was the old lady with her tiny wooden table and stools, trying to eke out a living selling tiny cups of green tea; the old toothless crone who guarded parked bikes for a small fee; and the small café owner who fastidiously swept the pavement and roadway in front of his shop every day. The street had its own unique soundtrack, too: the snip of the barber's scissors mixed with the sound of running water from the bike washers to soothe on hot summer afternoons, the call of the itinerant knife sharpener, the bread sellers advertising their hot fresh loaves, a mystery whistler heard just before dawn, the government loudspeakers issuing news and propaganda early each morning, the sound of Vietnamese love songs from a nearby karaoke room at night. After living there for almost three years, I ended up the very last person to leave the guesthouse when VNPT eventually took over the building for more office space.

Directly opposite my guesthouse was a large apartment block with small shops at street level and then three floors of apartments. This mouldering building, home and business to many families, seemed to undergo a continual metamorphosis, constantly adapting to swelling families and reflecting improved material conditions. In early 1994, none of the windows in the building had glass, only a wire grille with a drop-down clothes line and wooden louvre shutters. One apartment had a small cantilevered balcony and another had an attic and roof garden. Two years later, one third of the apartments had window-mounted airconditioners and glass, and the building effectively had another floor added to it as everyone living on the top floor extended up onto the roof. In addition, there were considerable lateral developments, with half-a-dozen cantilevered extensions of varying sizes, from modest balconies to multiple rooms. Now resembling an old beast covered by scabs and tumours, I worried that the building would just topple over from the additions, or else collapse if another hole was knocked into the external wall to add one more airconditioner or balcony.

Extended families were forced by economic circumstances to live in increasingly cramped conditions. Like many housing blocks, this building had no running water, only a public well and tap opposite where residents would bring tin dishes and do their washing by hand on the nearby pavement, or bring soap and towel and wash themselves in cold water, winter or summer. Yet each day I would see emerge from these poor conditions young schoolgirls in immaculate white traditional dress, known as *ao dai*, with shiny black hair held by fresh ribbons, young men with polished shoes and slicked-back hair looking freshly scrubbed, office workers and businessmen heading off in suits, complete with tiepins and briefcases.

Life is lived on the streets in Vietnam, no doubt because Vietnamese apartments are usually small and crowded, and often dark and uncomfortable, but also because the people like to be part of the crowd, to watch and interact and enjoy the company of others. On hot summer nights families sit outside to get some relief, children play together, chairs are brought out, sometimes televisions and fans are connected up with long leads, and there is always eating and drinking on the streets. Old men can be found playing chess and chequers, especially in the parks and around the lakes. Young men form huddled groups playing cards. In soccer season, all the young boys kick balls about. In kite-flying season, the sky is full of kites, and to my horror I found they were being flown from the rooftops. I was almost sick with worry when, day after day for several weeks when the winds were right, I saw children running back and forth on the roof of the apartment block opposite, amid a thick forest of television aerials, determined to get their new kites into the air.

Very early in the morning almost everyone goes off for some form of exercise before work. The area around Hoan Kiem Lake in the centre of the city is crowded with old people doing tai chi or other forms of gentle exercise. Lenin Park is jam-packed with all the badminton players from sunrise to about 8am, and other groups are off playing football or netball. Some of the women who need to stay near home form their own little exercise group and follow instructions from the loudspeakers nearby; '*mot, hai, ba*' (one, two, three) I would hear from the comfort of my bed early each morning.

Very soon I found that I enjoyed street life, too. I would eat at places the locals ate, which were set up on the pavement, in small laneways or in tiny rooms that were part of their home. While eating or drinking, I enjoyed watching the passing parade, the endless variety of life of the city, and almost always had a pleasant or interesting encounter—a conversation, an invitation, a compliment, an introduction. In the morning the street scene would build up slowly: sometimes the day would start with the squeal of a pig being slaughtered nearby, then the soup sellers would set up their tables and stools, bowls and chopsticks, and start boiling their cauldrons; the fresh meat sellers would be cutting up and displaying their wares; and next the fruit and vegetable sellers would arrive with their laden baskets of freshly picked produce carried on a shoulder pole, along with the bread sellers carrying their baskets of fresh hot rolls on their heads, and the sticky rice sellers carrying their wooden pails and calling their distinctive cry. As the housewives began their household chores, sweeping and putting their houses in order, the flower sellers arrived, bicycles overflowing with freshly cut flowers. All Vietnamese love flowers, keeping a vase of flowers on the family altar most of the time and giving them as gifts for most occasions. As the morning matured, the traffic increased and so too did the noise—car horns, bells on *cyclos* (the Vietnamese version of a rickshaw), barking dogs, children playing on their way to school, shops getting ready for business heralded by the sound of heavy metal security grills being pushed open. Sometimes you might hear voices raised in an argument; other times it might be the mournful sound of funeral music as someone's spirit is sent off at dawn.

At the end of the day, the street became quiet again as people went home to sleep. Then the street sweepers, usually women, came by, plying their large brooms and shovels, clearing away all the household rubbish, the food scraps and paper napkins from the food stalls, the hair from the barber's, the dead flowers. Night-time was also the time that building materials got delivered, that road work was undertaken, or that illegal water connections were made. I have been woken by the sounds of a truck-load of brick and gravel being dumped, by the flash of welding throughout the night where workmen have been constructing a complete spiral metal staircase and roof balcony, and by the sound of the road being dug up outside my window as a family lay a pipeline right across the road to connect to a water main.

Over the years I became quite attached to my modest little room at the guesthouse, telling my Western friends that I was enjoying a minimalist period. My Vietnamese friends, on the other hand, would marvel at the luxury I enjoyed—a whole room to myself! My first room measured about 5 x 3.5 metres and contained a king-size wooden bed, bedside table and reading lamp, wooden wardrobe, a wooden desk and chair, two unpadded wooden armchairs, a coffee table, television and small fridge. Before I arrived, my friends had instructed the guesthouse staff to arrange it 'like a lady's bedroom'. The floor was tiled, the ceiling high and there were huge gaps in the wooden door and window frames, which let in the icy winds in winter and the mosquitoes in summer. The airconditioner only cooled and did so with a lot of chugging, punctuated by deep sighs as it cut in and out. Nevertheless, after about a week I became used to its womb noises and found them positively soothing. Its rumblings also helped to mask the buzzing of the fluorescent lights during the day and the geckos' mating squeals during the night.

The bathroom was quite large with toilet, basin, mirror and shelf, and a 'free-range' shower—a shower head attached to the wall so that everything in the room got wet. However, once I got a system in place and learned where to put my towel and other items, I began to quite enjoy the freedom from the constraints of a conventional shower recess. When I moved to the room next door after eighteen months, the bathroom was much the same, but the main room was bigger, about 5 x 5 metres, and I had another tiny room with a tiled bench where I could put an electric kettle and plug-in hotplate—almost a kitchen! Also with this room came a three-piece wooden lounge suite with red vinyl cushions and, best of all, a reverse-cycle airconditioner; no more huddling in bed in my overcoat during the cold damp Hanoi winters. And like my old room, this one also had a balcony from where I could watch my neighbourhood world.

The guesthouse staff changed the bed sheets and bath towels regularly, and they would have done my personal washing if I had wanted, but I decided that I could be responsible for at least that chore. I had two large dishes for washing, and little else to do in the way of domestic chores since I didn't cook or clean, so each night my free-range shower would double as a washing room. I became close to the guesthouse staff over the years. Miss Chi, who helped me pay bills, arrange newspaper delivery and provide advice on how to do most things, was twenty-nine years old then and worried about being left on the shelf. Miss Thu and Miss Nga were younger and were both keen to improve their English, taking every opportunity to practise speaking to me, their only native English-speaking resident. Miss Nga, in particular, liked to impress me with her vocabulary, describing someone as 'punctilious' or 'supercilious', or the Hanoi weather as 'capricious'. Because of their past isolation and lack of up-to-date books, many of the expressions Vietnamese used sounded quaintly outdated, like calling a high-ranking person a 'big potato', or describing someone as their 'bosom friend'.

Most days Nga could be heard singing as she worked, with a voice so sweet but surprisingly strong, coming from such a tiny body. Yet she had little in life to sing about. Nga's father had died some years before and her mother was not strong and so, since she had a younger sister and brother, Nga had to be the main breadwinner of the family, which meant giving up her aspirations for higher education. Before working at the guesthouse (where in 1994 she earned just US$1 a day) she had spent a few years in the former Soviet Union as part of a cheap labour scheme. However, her hopes of saving money so she could study were thwarted with the abrupt political upheaval in Eastern Europe, leaving Nga destitute over there and unable to return to Vietnam for a while. The conditions she endured there, and the long hours and hard work, have had a long-term effect on her health but, incredibly, not on her spirit.

Life in Hanoi was too interesting for me to care too much about decorating my room in the guesthouse. But on a visit back to Australia for Christmas, I discovered glow-in-the-dark stick-on stars: one hundred and twenty-six tiny, tiny stars with a few planets, moons and comets. It was quite a job getting them stuck on the ceiling of my room. I had no ladder and had to balance each tiny star on the end of a long piece of bamboo and push it onto the high ceiling. Originally I had plans of recreating the complete southern constellation, but the procedure was so difficult that after making a part of a Southern Cross, I gave up and just stuck them anywhere. But it was well worth the few hours it took, especially for the looks on the staff's faces when I showed them. Quite unwittingly, however, I gave poor Mr Hung, who was on duty at reception that night, a bit of a shock. Without thinking carefully about how it might be interpreted, I raced downstairs, grabbed Mr Hung by the hand and said, 'Come up to my room, I want to show you something.' Warily, he followed me and when we reached my room I told him to lie down on my bed while I turned the lights out. 'Look at the ceiling, look at the ceiling,' I shouted when I saw the look of incredulous terror in his eyes, finally realising how this situation could have appeared.

I loved my time at the Post Office Guesthouse. I got used to curtains held on by bulldog clips, and Bulgarian electric kettles that could sometimes fling you across the room, or finding Nga asleep on my lounge, too tired to finish cleaning my room. Even the power cuts—which also meant no water because the pump wouldn't work—weren't too bad. Everyone else was suffering, and it was a good reminder that most people never had running water or airconditioning. At least when the lights went out I always had someone there to share their candle and pass the time with until the power was restored. And I enjoyed a sense of community—people to say hello to, to complain about the weather to, who complimented me if I wore something special, who told me about their children, who noticed if I went away and when I returned. When I would hang my Vietnamese flag on my balcony to celebrate national holidays, I would receive the approving nods of my neighbours opposite. Once I was at a restaurant and the waitress told me she recognised me because her family lived opposite me. 'We all think you are an interesting woman,' she told me, making me realise just how much my life was on display.

The other great advantage of living in the guesthouse was the constant coming and going of guests. Some I already knew as ex-students, or from my visits to Ho Chi Minh City, Da Nang, Nha Trang or other towns. Others I got to know from their frequent visits. In no time it seemed I knew just about every director, deputy director or technical expert of every provincial post office in the country, since at some time each year they had to pay a visit to VNPT headquarters in Hanoi. Often they would invite me to visit their province, and while in Hanoi would invite me to karaoke or dinner, or even breakfast, so I never lacked company. Three staff from Lang Son province used to come to Hanoi once a month to study at the university, and on one trip, invited Miss Thu and me to go back with them for a two-day holiday, where they showed us around and then sent us back to Hanoi in the mail van. A Chinese professor once stayed at the guesthouse for a couple of weeks and afterwards arranged an invitation for me to visit his university at Nanjing in China.

When I finally moved into a house I found it difficult to get used to having a lot of living space again. I would tend to perch on my bed, like a caged bird finally let out into the wild but not knowing what to do with so much freedom. And I missed my guesthouse family, and my neighbours, and the sounds of my street. How much I had changed since that April day in 1994 when I first drove up to 11b Tran Quoc Toan Street and thought that the quality of my life was about to take a severe tumble when, in fact, I was about to enjoy an enrichment I couldn't have imagined.

Mrs Thanh and the fortune teller

It was Alexander, a Russian from Vladivostok studying linguistics at Hanoi University, who introduced me to Mrs Thanh, and it was she who took me to my first fortune teller in Hanoi. I had met Alexander on the way to my first Vietnamese language class at Hanoi University. A couple of days later our paths crossed once more, and in the course of our conversation, Alexander suggested that I meet his friend, Mrs Thanh, who would teach me Vietnamese in exchange for English lessons. And so we arranged for the three of us to meet for dinner, a chance encounter leading to an enduring friendship and the start of a number of adventures initiated by Mrs Thanh. It was Mrs Thanh who pushed me off to ballroom dancing, Mrs Thanh who, with her friend Mrs Thu, plotted to find me a husband, and Mrs Thanh who introduced me to Mr Hanh, a Vietnamese fortune teller specialising in Chinese astrology.

At our first meeting Mrs Thanh was so shy she could barely speak to me. I learnt that she had taught herself English from a dictionary, which meant she could read and write but found speaking and listening difficult as she had little opportunity to practise these skills. Alexander had been helping her, with the result that when she tried to speak English it was with a thick Russian accent (which I would later overlay with flat Australian vowels). Yet despite the difficulties, Mrs Thanh's hunger for knowledge and desire to communicate with a Western woman overrode her fears, and whenever she had time she would pedal her ancient green Chinese bicycle to my place and laboriously explain various aspects of Vietnamese culture, ways of thinking and attitudes—often resorting to her dictionary or drawings and diagrams—and question me closely about Western views and customs.

Mrs Thanh had spent some time in Moscow studying at university and now, in her mid-forties, was professor of linguistics at Hanoi University and soon to complete her doctorate. She had two sons, and had divorced her husband a few years before I met her. Divorce was still unusual in Hanoi and Vietnam generally, especially for someone who was concerned about maintaining the social conventions of conservative Hanoi society. I discovered that Mrs Thanh enjoyed living vicariously through me, suggesting places I should go and even what I should wear. 'I am a Party Member and a university professor. I have two sons. Therefore I can do nothing!' she would lament. 'But you are a Western woman, alone in a foreign country; you can do anything!' The Vietnamese view of Westerners has been gleaned from communist propaganda and, more recently, from pirated copies of Hollywood movies, resulting in a picture of hedonism and promiscuity. Mrs Thanh was a little disappointed that my life wasn't more colourful and racy, but over the months and years of our conversations we found a real closeness and more similarities than differences, as we compared our marriages, divorces and children, and exchanged stories about our friends.

One day Mrs Thanh told me about some friends who had been to visit a fortune teller in Hanoi and how they had been impressed with the accuracy of the revelations. She had some difficulty coming to terms with such irrational and unscientific beliefs, but at the same time was attracted to the idea. Eventually she found a compromise, telling me with a cheeky grin, 'As a Party Member and professor, I believe in Marxist Leninism, but only 75 per cent, leaving 25 per cent to the gods.' She decided to conduct a scientific experiment by going to two different fortune tellers and cross-checking them, and set some traps by telling some half-truths on subsequent visits. However, as it turned out, their consistency and capacity to see through her fabrications gave both of us food for thought. By now I was intrigued and we decided that I should go to see Mr Hanh, who practiced Chinese astrology, with Mrs Thanh acting as my interpreter, to see if fortune telling as practised in Vietnam would work for foreigners.

Mr Hanh lived about ten kilometres from the centre of Hanoi, and since Mrs Thanh only owned a bicycle, we each hired a motorbike taxi to take us there. Mr Hanh's house was extremely modest, even by Vietnamese standards—just a room with a wooden bed on one side, a long wooden lounge where we sat, a coffee table in front of us, and opposite, an old cane chair where he sat next to some shelves containing some dusty ancient-looking books. On the wall behind Mr Hanh was a shelf holding a small family altar with fresh flowers, incense and photos of his ancestors. Next to this room on one side was a hairdressing salon, clearly visible through a large opening in the wall; on the other side was a rickety lean-to where Mr Hanh's family sold refreshments and which probably also served as the family kitchen.

The Vietnamese government tries to discourage fortune telling and other superstitious practices, but this wasn't the reason Mr Hanh had some reservations about seeing me. He was worried whether his methodology would work with a foreigner. He only required a person's name and date and time of birth, but in my case he had to take account of the time difference between Hanoi and Sydney, and the difference of hemisphere, where January was the middle of summer and not the middle of winter as he was used to. He also told Mrs Thanh that, for some reason I never worked out, he was concerned that he wasn't familiar with the plants and animals of Australia. And he had to also check out equivalent letters, since the Vietnamese alphabet lacks some of our consonants and has extra vowels. This was going to be a test of Mr Hanh's skills, and because I couldn't understand what he was saying, he wouldn't be receiving any feedback from me.

Mrs Thanh busily took notes and occasionally she would give me a brief summary or check some point with me. At first Mr Hanh's observations were quite general—accurate as far as they went, but not proof for a cynic. As he continued, however, his reading of past events became more and more specific and detailed. At one stage I had to shake some metal coins in a special way, give him a sequence of numbers, and manipulate cards. He would consult his books and papers and sometimes perform calculations on a small plastic-covered, battery-operated calculator. After more than an hour, it seemed as if he would keep talking forever. I was getting concerned about Mrs Thanh who had already filled six pages with notes, about our motorbike taxi drivers who were waiting outside, and about the other customers waiting their turn. However, Mr Hanh was very relaxed and unperturbed, and the flow of words seemed effortless. At one point while in full verbal flight, he picked up an old pair of scissors and unselfconsciously began to trim his fingernails, then moved to his toenails. Was this part of the ritual, I wondered? Like reading the entrails of chickens, perhaps? No, just long nails apparently! In the next room we could clearly see a customer having her hair washed and cut. On the other side, some locals had gathered for tea, and there were assorted children and animals hanging around to take a look and listen to the fortunes of this foreign woman who had come to consult their local oracle. For those waiting their turn, it must have been like an episode out of a television soap opera. And to add a bit more drama, at one point a neighbour rushed in seeking an urgent consultation. It seemed that someone in her family had recently died 'at a bad time', although I am not sure when a good time to die would be. Apparently this meant that someone else in the family would die within six months if nothing was done to avert this second death in some way. Mr Hanh gave her some advice and something written on paper, and without missing a beat was back onto my life and fortune. The audience used the lull to interrogate Mrs Thanh about me, filling in any bits of information they may have missed.

After two hours and eight pages of notes Mrs Thanh looked exhausted. When I asked about payment, Mr Hanh didn't want to accept anything, but Mrs Thanh told me to give him US$2, which was two or three times what a Vietnamese person would usually pay. The following day, Mrs Thanh went through the notes she had taken with me, filling in the sketchy outline she had given me at the time. The accuracy of his observations was astounding: the description of characteristics, past events and even the position of moles and description of a tooth of my son. Even without the benefit of later verification of his predictions, I was impressed. How did he do it? Mrs Thanh said it came from years of studying Chinese books, not any supernatural powers. Mr Hanh clearly saw it as a science and vocation, and he certainly wasn't getting rich from its practice. Needless to say, Mrs Thanh and I were now hooked and we made a number of trips to Mr Hanh and other fortune tellers over the next six or seven years.

There was another well-known fortune teller in Hanoi—Mr Tu, a young man who, on recovering from a serious accident where he almost died, discovered a psychic ability. Tu lived near the centre of Hanoi in the middle of a confusing rabbit warren of narrow lanes. He asked no information, only requiring that you bring a betel nut and leaf with you. (I usually bought mine from a nearby market, much to the surprise of the old Vietnamese woman selling them, who one day asked my friend if I was Vietnamese! With blue eyes and fair hair and skin!) Tu would place the betel nut on a small plate and slice it in half, then concentrate on the leaf and begin to talk. As I got to know him better over the years, I asked what fortune telling was like for him, and he explained that he heard voices in his head telling him the information that he merely passed on, uncensored. There was no hesitation in the flow of Tu's words and it appeared effortless. At times he might be interrupted, or stop to make himself a cup of tea, but he would immediately pick up where he had left off, as if a pause button had been pushed then released. Interestingly, it was said that as his health improved over the years, his powers began to decline.

Once some of my other Vietnamese women friends learnt of my interest in fortune tellers, they were keen to take me to others they had heard about. One morning Mrs Nga picked me up on her motorbike at 5.30am. We rode for an hour through torrential rain, slipping and sliding on the muddy roads on our way to a tiny village of just a handful of homes, where we found lots of chickens, geese and bare-bottomed children running about. The fortune teller who lived there was reputed to give advice to some members of the government, so was highly sought after, which was why we had to go there so early—before he had eaten his breakfast as it turned out. We waited outside his yard until just after 7am, by which time quite a few more people were lined up to see him. We were finally ushered in to his small and modest room and without any preliminary questions, he laughed as he told my friend (extremely accurately and in detail) what her problems were and how to overcome them. He was a little suspicious of me (a result of not having had contact with Westerners because he was a 'countryside person' and not a more sophisticated Hanoian, according to my friend) but he did give me some timely advice about moving to a new house with a north-east facing gate.

Generally, most fortune tellers were delighted to have the opportunity to test their skills on a foreigner and I found myself taken to a variety of places and giving my time of birth, or manipulating cards or coins or sticks, and hearing through my interpreter what my future held. Some of the advice didn't always translate well across cultural differences. I don't know what my children would have made of it if I had requested them, as advised, to 'Renovate our ancestral tomb and build a small pagoda, and release a small fish into a lake on the first and fifteenth day of each lunar month before saying prayers,' to help me through a bad year. But I did follow a fortune teller's advice when my son had some problems, going to a particular pagoda where I asked the *bonze* (monk) to perform a special ceremony for him according to some written instructions my interpreter had given me. I had to give the pagoda some money for special fruit and incense and then attend on the correct day and sit cross-legged on the floor for more than an hour as the women of the pagoda, led by the chief *bonze*, chanted and prayed. My son was not impressed by my efforts, but his problems disappeared!

When I talked with my Vietnamese friends about the potential danger of relying on or worrying too much about what was predicted, Mrs Thanh explained that even bad news can be accepted positively, with the right attitude. If, for example, you are told of some bad luck or misfortune, you can usually gain some comfort from knowing that later there will be good luck, or that your bad luck may be preventing some worse suffering, or at least from knowing that nothing can be done, if that is what the gods will. Once I was told I would not have any success that year, but if that wasn't the case, someone in my family would die, thereby making me grateful for my small misfortunes. Maybe this idea of stoic acceptance accounts for the Vietnamese strength.

I learned many valuable lessons from Mrs Thanh. Once, when I was away from Hanoi for a couple of months, she wrote to me: 'When I go back home from my working place in the evening, I always look up to the sky, the moon, the stars, and sing. I find happiness from everybody, from everywhere. I am satisfied with what I have now.' One day she told me that she always tries to extract the maximum enjoyment from the moment. 'If I am sitting here with you drinking tea,' she explained, 'then that is what I want to be doing and I feel happy. I don't think about being somewhere else or wish I was doing something else. I just take pleasure in being here and doing this.'

One of the weirdest experiences I shared with Mrs Thanh was the day she took me to the woman who, it was said, could summon and communicate with the dead. Her friend, Mr Kim, had been the week before and said that he had talked to his dead father, and the things that were communicated were accurate and convincing. Now Mrs Thanh wanted to check it out—in the spirit of further scientific inquiry, she explained to me as she tried to keep the excitement out of her voice.

We set off on motorbike taxis to an address near the major dyke on the Red River. We could see a lot of people outside a two-storey house and others standing on the upper balcony. We made our way inside and up the stairs to a large room dominated by an altar and filled to capacity with people sitting quietly on the floor. Near the centre of the room, a young woman, dressed very simply like a peasant, was sitting on a mat on the floor, and near her was an older well-dressed and heavily made-up woman, wearing gold chains and bracelets, who clearly managed the business and collected payment. In order to make contact you needed to supply the name of the deceased, the date of their death, their age when they died and where they are buried. Two coins were thrown into a small saucer and if they both showed heads, that meant contact was possible.

The young woman medium wafted some incense in her face, then covered her face with her hands and slowly swayed, finally falling backwards and needing to be caught. Then she began to speak, apparently with the voice of the person summoned. Everyone in the room was transfixed by what was happening.

I felt so frustrated at not being able to follow everything being said, having to rely on Mrs Thanh to translate. But even without understanding the meaning of the words, I could hear the different voices and distinguish different 'persona'. When a child was contacted, the medium spoke with a childlike voice and her body moved in childlike ways, twisting her fingers and even crying when she talked about how sad she was because her home had been taken away. At this point there were murmurs in the audience: they wanted to know what it meant and if it was accurate. 'Yes', the parents told them. 'The child's tomb was removed to make way for a building'. A gasp passed though the crowd and heads nodded in agreement.

The next person contacted was clearly a man. After falling into her trance, this time the medium sat up, asked for a cigarette and proceeded to smoke it, holding it like a man would. Her body movements and voice, too, were very different. Mrs Thanh was hooked and, even with only partial understanding, so was I! We stayed there listening and watching for more than an hour, mesmerised, until the woman in charge asked Mrs Thanh if I would like to contact someone. Vietnamese are invariably polite and generous to foreigners, and while I always felt embarrassed at being given preferential treatment, no-one seemed to resent this blatant queue-jumping. Later, we found out that some people there had travelled hundreds of kilometres and had been waiting their turn since the day before, and most had been queued up since 4am that morning. Mrs Thanh had no scruples, however: here was an opportunity for her scientific research. Unfortunately, I didn't know the details of any family members who had died but, like all Vietnamese, Mrs Thanh could supply all the required details on her father, so it was agreed that she would try to contact him and I would sit next to her and observe.

First we had to go downstairs and buy some items—paper gold and silver, paper money and incense—and burn them and say prayers. (It is believed that burning paper replicas of material comforts can transport those comforts to the deceased in the afterlife. Paper representing gold, silver and currency—invariably US dollars—is the most common offering, but there are paper Honda motorbikes, Mercedes cars, televisions and even paper human partners in case the departed gets lonely.) Then we went back upstairs and gave all the necessary particulars to the medium, who fell into a swoon in my lap. Immediately, she began to make choking noises, which alarmed me, especially when I saw the expression of fear and incredulity on Mrs Thanh's face. Then the choking suddenly stopped and she began to move the pillow under her head, trying to fold it in half to make it higher. Next, one of her legs seemed to become cramped and twisted and she kept rubbing at it. Mrs Thanh was so clearly affected by this that she was unable to explain to me what was happening at the time, and I had to wait until we were outside to understand the significance of what we had witnessed. Mrs Thanh told me her father had died while eating a meal and hence the choking; that he had a habit of folding his pillow in half; and that she always used to massage his leg, which would become stiff and immovable in exactly the way the woman had depicted.

Nothing was said during this initial enactment, but it clearly established in Mrs Thanh's mind that it was indeed her father who had been contacted. The first words he spoke through the medium were to complain that he had been called unexpectedly. The correct procedure is to pray at the family altar and make special preparations before making the summons, but because it was unplanned, Mrs Thanh had not gone through the correct steps. Later, I wondered what he was so busy doing that he objected to an interruption! He also talked about being cold and wanting his special thick jacket, which, Mrs Thanh told me, was the only piece of clothing the family had kept after he died. My literal Western brain was wrestling with the problem of how she could get this jacket to him, when Mrs Thanh said impatiently, 'You burn a paper replica, of course!' When she asked his permission to go to Malaysia to work, he agreed, giving her instructions about praying at the family tomb before going. And then our time was up.

Outside, Mrs Thanh explained everything to me and we were both nonplussed. Our logical, scientific minds couldn't accept what we had seen and heard, and yet we couldn't find an alternative explanation. There was never any hesitation in the speech of the medium; she always talked fluently and remained completely in character. We never went back there, although we talked about it often, and I have added it to a number of other things I experienced in Vietnam that I will never understand. But I have told Mrs Thanh that if I die before her, she is to call me—but making sure she gives me the correct notice first!

Cumquats and zoot suits: celebrating the lunar new year

When I think of Tet, the annual Vietnamese festival for the lunar new year, I remember the ones I celebrated when I first went to live in Hanoi. I had moved there just after the last Tet when fireworks were allowed. Expatriate friends had told me how lucky I was to have missed that experience. According to them, it was like living in a city under siege—the air thick with smoke for days, the noise keeping everyone awake night after night, and it was actually quite dangerous to go out in the streets when firecrackers were being thrown everywhere. Every year vast numbers of people were injured, some seriously maimed and even killed. But to most Vietnamese this was the way Tet had always been celebrated and always should be. When the government finally decided to ban fireworks, young and old mourned the decision, and those villages that relied entirely on firework production for their income had to find other acceptable income-producing activities.

In Tet of 1995, the Year of the Pig, a few diehards defied the government and occasional sounds of fireworks could be heard, usually at night. But the severity of the penalties, including long jail terms, and the vigilance of the police soon put a stop to it. The police service's work was made more difficult, however, by the rather novel solution some entrepreneur had come up with of having taped fireworks noises. The following year, the Year of the Rat, the selling and playing of these tapes was also banned, leaving Vietnamese no alternative but to celebrate Tet in silence, except for the government's public fireworks displays.

Tet is a bit like Christmas and the Western celebration of the new year rolled into one. Falling around January or February, it symbolises a new beginning with the ushering in of spring, and is a time for family reunions and new clothes, for visiting friends and for fulfilling obligations to ancestors and placating the gods. Traditional foods are prepared, children are given small gifts or money in red envelopes, and homes are spruced up and decorated with a cumquat tree or peach blossom, or sometimes both.

Miss Thuy, a young colleague from the VNPT, arrived on her motorbike early on the Saturday before my first Tet to take me to the main flower market in Hanoi. The streets were overflowing with trees and blossoms, and as thousands were sold more would arrive in *cyclos*, on bicycles, in small vans, pulled along on trolleys or just carried; the city was like a huge moving garden. Despite the vast array from which to chose, Miss Thuy couldn't find a tree exactly to her liking at the market, so we rode to the famous gardens near West Lake where many Tet trees are grown.

Great care is taken over the selection of a Tet tree. A peach blossom branch must have aesthetic proportions, must have the right number of blossoms and not be too mature otherwise all the blossoms will have dropped before the end of the Tet season. Above all, it should ideally reflect something about the personality of the buyer. Some customers order their trees or branches a year in advance and may even have it shaped and trimmed to their specifications by experts in this field. Others look for the unique in nature, without human intervention.

Miss Thuy wanted a cumquat tree, but it had to be the right size to suit her room and it had to have a good symmetrical shape with a mixture of green fruit, orange fruit, fresh new pale green leaves and some small white flowers. After an extensive search driving up and down Nhat Tan Road, she finally spotted the one she wanted, and after some haggling we carried off our prize specimen for a little less than US$3. Bringing it home balanced on the back of her motorbike with my face pressed against the foliage made me feel like a real local—as did helping her to carry it up five flights of stairs to her apartment!

That New Year's Eve I was invited to a small party in a Vietnamese home where we drank Russian champagne from Bohemian crystal glasses and ate traditional Tet food including *banh chung,* made from green-coloured glutinous rice and stuffed with pork fat, beans and shallots then wrapped in banana leaves. At about 11.30pm everyone headed for Hoan Kiem Lake in the centre of Hanoi to enjoy the fireworks display, calling in to an old pagoda on the way home to say the first prayers of the new year and light some incense for good luck.

On the morning of the first day of the new lunar year, the streets are strangely quiet. The first visitor to the home is very important and is believed to determine the fortunes of the family for the coming year. Those believed to bring good luck are in high demand; men are preferred over women, and the richer and more successful they are, the better. Most families don't leave it to chance, and as a precaution against some harbinger of bad luck stumbling through their door, they arrange for a family member to become the first visitor or 'first-footer' soon after midnight. Vietnamese weren't quite sure about foreigners to begin with. We looked prosperous, as if the gods had smiled upon us, but we were an unknown quantity and so initially were kept away from the duties of being 'first-footer', since no-one was sure how the gods would react. But over the years attitudes changed, and in 2000 I was invited to be 'first-footer' at my friend Minh's house, an honour but also a worrying responsibility, and I must say I was relieved when the year ended without any misfortune raining down upon the family.

These days, although it isn't exactly business as usual during Tet, there are at least enough eating places open for tourists and expatriates to survive. But it wasn't always so, and since my room at the guesthouse where I first lived didn't have cooking facilities, I was grateful for the invitations I received to celebrate Tet with Vietnamese friends at their homes—even though it meant trying to swallow yet another piece of *banh chung* or some tough chicken, or down another toast in rice wine under often bizarre circumstances. Over the years my invitations were many and varied, covering a broad range of social and economic situations: a *cyclo* driver's family, a training centre director, a noodle seller, the director of a government department, a teacher, a doctor, guesthouse cleaners, an engineer, a waiter's family.

Not far from my guesthouse, every afternoon at about 5.30pm, a woman in her thirties would set up her small tables and stools on the pavement, start heating her huge cauldron and pile up on a table next to her a mountain of uncooked noodles, twenty-two cooked chickens and assorted bowls of chicken claws, hearts, livers and other innards. And there she would stay until about 3am or later, serving the most delicious chicken noodle soup, or *pho ga*, in Hanoi for about 50 cents. She did a roaring trade, with some young assistants to serve, cut up lemons and garnish, clear tables and wash up in the gutter nearby. Lit by bare globes strung along the wall of the adjacent building, it always looked inviting, especially on cold winter's nights with the steam rising as everyone huddled over their bowls. If it started to rain, the helpers would drag out a large piece of heavy plastic and somehow suspend it over the tables using bamboo and bits of string and wire. If the rain was very heavy or prolonged, the plastic would sag dangerously until someone came along and gave it a prod, resulting in a cascade of water and often a few damp diners.

What I didn't realise at first was that Mrs Noodles, as I referred to her, was part of an emerging breed of small-time entrepreneurs. She mightn't have studied at business school, but she understood and had all the elements for success: a good location where there were locals and foreigners, a product that was consistently good and suited to both local and foreign tastes, being open at the right time, and while not the cheapest in town, her meals were very good value for money. Over the years I saw her success unfold so that these days, though she still has some tables on the pavement for al fresco dining, now she has expanded into the ground floor of the building where she used to string her lights and it is full of her smart new tables, along with a proper cooking area and fridges. And she has someone else to cook the chickens and noodles, to supervise the waiters and stay up late, while she and her husband keep a general eye on things and count the profits.

I was a regular customer in her early years, but even so, I was a little surprised to be invited to visit her home for Tet. I was told that one of the boys who worked for her would take me there on his motorbike. Oddly, I never saw Mrs Noodles herself on the day, only her husband. And I am not sure if it was even their house I ended up at, or the house of a neighbour or family member. It was a freezing day and I was ushered in to the living area of what seemed a new home, sat down on a new vinyl lounge, still with its plastic covering, and plied with whisky, beer and lollies while the neighbourhood kids stared and giggled in the doorway. Then a photographer arrived and I was posed next to the huge peach blossom for photos with various combinations of people who appeared. Next, they turned on the television and video and played me a Bony M concert, vintage 1970s judging by the clothes and hair. Finally it was over and I was ready to make my escape, but now I was told that as the final treat of my Tet visit, my motorbike driver would take me for a ride through Lenin Park before dropping me back home—never mind that the temperature was 6°C with high humidity and a wind that chilled to the bone despite heavy layering of woollens and gloves. Clearly they had pulled out all stops for me, and somehow it had given them pleasure.

Another Tet, I was invited to visit the home of a young waiter named Hung whom I had helped buy a bicycle so that he could work the long hours necessary to keep his restaurant job but still live at home. His mother wanted to thank me, so Hung arrived at my guesthouse to escort me to his home. Since I didn't think I could manage being doubled on a bicycle, I hired a *cyclo* and Hung rode alongside, and we maneuvered our way through a maze of twisting and turning laneways that were cold, dank and dirty. I was taken inside his tiny dilapidated house to find his stepfather, dressed in pyjamas, lying on the lounge looking very ill and with a consumptive cough. His mother, sitting on a thin woven mat on the floor, looked old and worn.

We had tea and some special Tet sweets, and I was running out of polite small talk when I hit on the idea of taking a photo as a prelude to leaving. This suggestion caused a flurry of excitement and galvanised the whole family into action. The stepfather rose from his sickbed, whipped a suit out of the cupboard and went off behind a curtain to change, returning all decked out, complete with tiepin and hat! Meanwhile Hung's mother grabbed her *ao dai* from the cupboard, a sparkly ribbon for her hair and some beads to wear around her neck. Not to be outdone, Hung pulled a small trench coat from somewhere and insisted on wearing dark glasses, obviously satisfying some detective fantasy of his.

Of course I was delighted with their obvious pleasure and realised that sadly they had no camera of their own to record their lives and special times. We take so many things for granted in our privileged society! Then just as everyone had finished dressing up, I was amazed to find a young woman and small child, both of them dressed to the nines with lots of make-up, coming down ladder-like steps from an attic room. They turned out to be the daughter of Hung's stepfather and her little girl, apparently lured out of the attic by the promise of a photo. By this time I had lost control of the situation, and Hung's stepfather, who had seemed so frail before, was now directing the operation, requesting various positions and poses, some serious expressions, some head-only shots. The daughter was concerned with getting her new shoes into the picture—not an easy request since the room was small and she was tall, so we had to compromise and have her seated with her legs crossed so the shoes could be seen. Seventeen photos later, the film mercifully ran out! And I could happily make my escape.

In 1997, loud check 'zoot suits' were the Tet fashion craze for little boys, and everywhere these miniature men's suits with matching shirt and tie could be seen hanging outside all the clothing shops. An Australian couple and I had been invited to Mr Kim's house, a close friend of Mrs Thanh and my sometime dancing partner, for what we understood was afternoon tea, since we had explained to him we already had a lunch engagement that day. When we arrived at his rather grand house overlooking Hoan Kiem Lake, we were greeted by Mr Kim, looking resplendent in his cream double-breasted suit, and his ten-year-old son in a brown and cream checked suit, and led to a banquet that had been prepared for us. It was only 2.30pm, not long enough for us to have digested our enormous lunchtime feast; however, we tried to put on a brave front. My friend's husband, who admittedly resembles Santa Claus more than Gandhi, was doing his best to reduce the mountain of food before us when Mr Kim's zoot-suited son came over to him, poked at his stomach and said, in perfect English, 'fat'! Although my friend laughed it off with a rather strained smile at the time, he later complained indignantly about the injustice of being plied with unwanted food and then criticised for the outcome.

In recent years on New Year's Eve a big concert has been held outside Hanoi's magnificent Opera House. The surrounding roads are blocked to traffic and are instead packed with people. The entertainment includes traditional music, songs and dance as well as the latest in pop and rap. At midnight the fireworks display at Hoan Kiem Lake lights up the night sky. It always feels special to be part of a huge crowd where everyone is enjoying themselves and where the mood is relaxed, happy and full of goodwill. What I used to look forward to at Tet was walking around Hoan Kiem Lake to see the photographers trying to attract customers. Throughout the year there are a few permanent photographers based at this iconic Hanoi scenic spot, ready to snap visitors and locals. Customers can choose maybe a garlanded arch to stand under, or a toy car or rocking horse for their child, a large soft toy or a floral backdrop for their photo. But at Tet, dozens of photographers set up their stalls all along the edge of the lake and each tries to outdo the other in artistry, with larger-than-life-size models of the relevant animal of the Vietnamese lunar calendar.

The year 2000 was a big one. Not only was it a new millennium but also the Year of the Dragon, and there were scores of dragons to choose from: golden dragons, ones with flashing red eyes, large ones and small ones displaying varying degrees of artistic competence. After a full circuit to check out which dragon we liked the best, my friend Minh and I finally made our selection—a long fiery red dragon with lotus plants as a backdrop. The next day when we collected our print we complained to the photographer that we were not in focus. 'Yes,' he replied, 'but see how beautiful the dragon looks!'

The next year, the Year of the Snake, Minh and I found a rather cute coiled snake wearing a bowler hat and small round glasses, and this time we were all in focus. It was hard to find a decent-looking horse in 2002, Year of the Horse; some looked a bit like recycled dragons we remembered from two years earlier. We settled for a large white steed with disproportionately short legs, a sway-back, mad red eyes, and an open mouth showing about fifty white and even teeth. Minh sat up front for the photograph, with me side-saddle behind him, looking like something out of a twisted fairy tale! The photo done, we headed off for West Lake, another favourite spot of Hanoians over the Tet holiday. West Lake is enormous, so the first time that Minh said we would hire a boat and go rowing there, I imagined a relaxed afternoon away from the crowds and noise of the city, taking in the scenery as we drifted along. The reality was somewhat different: a small yellow rubber dinghy with a low plastic stool to sit on and tiny oars, and movement restricted to a few hundred metres from shore. If you overran the boundaries marked by buoys, a motorboat would round you up and send you back. And so we tied up to one of the marker buoys and bobbed about for forty-five minutes before rowing back to the hiring jetty. And that was our special Tet outing!

As Vietnam has become more prosperous, consumerism has overtaken communism as the leading ideology and Tet celebrations have taken on a distinctly commercial flavour. Once, the best most families could do to prepare their home for Tet was slap a new coat of cheap whitewash on the walls and maybe buy a new floor mat or bed mat. These days preparations are often much more extravagant; the pavements outside the electrical shops are full of the latest giant plasma screen televisions, high-quality sound systems, fridges, washing machines, microwaves, all waiting to be loaded for delivery. There are traffic jams in Carpet Street, and clothing shops and tailors are jam-packed with shoppers buying their new Tet clothes. The simple traditional Tet foods have now been supplemented with (and even supplanted by) a range of expensive foreign products, including special imported biscuits and chocolates, wines and spirits, exotic foods, perfumes and beauty products, often pre-packaged in gift hampers—a long way from the simple plastic trays of lotus seeds, dried fruits and seeds of old.

Yet, despite the increasing commercialism of Tet, for now, the traditional ways and values, the goodwill and hospitality still remain. It is still possible to turn your back on all the trendy new restaurants, bars, cafés and discos that overflow with the new affluent middle classes and the spoilt children of the cadres. I like to remember the simple celebrations: sitting with my friend on a tiny wooden stool on the footpath sipping a local Hanoi beer, sold to us by an almost toothless old man as the crowds milled around us and fireworks burst into the night sky, then going to eat a bowl of thick chicken rice soup before heading to the pagoda. That is the real Tet in Hanoi.

Hung the *cyclo* driver

There was no reason to think I would ever see Hung again after that first meeting during a short business trip to Hanoi in 1993. Yet over the next eight years I was to share, in a small way, his joys and sorrows and the more ordinary ups and downs of his life.

Vietnam had opened its doors in 1986. At first only a trickle of curious foreigners came to take a peep inside, then came various snake oil salesmen and 'cowboys' looking for a quick buck. By 1993 the trickle had become a stream, and between 1994 and 1996 Vietnam was 'flavour of the month' internationally, and foreign companies big and small beat a path to its nervously held open door.

Hung was a *cyclo* driver whose 'patch' was outside the Army Guesthouse. Back in 1993, the Army Guesthouse was where most foreign travellers stayed in Hanoi, unless they were diplomats, government ministers or rich French, in which case they often stayed at the overpriced Metropole Hotel. And given that in 1993 there were no taxis in town, no motorbike taxis and no public transport, the *cyclo* business was booming for those who could manage to get foreign passengers, who paid many times the amount paid by locals for being pedalled through the streets. *Cyclos* are like a rickshaw but with a Vietnamese twist—your driver, or pedaller, sits behind and above you. This provides you with an uninterrupted view of where you are going—not always welcomed when it seems that where you are going is straight into an oncoming truck!

After checking into the Army Guesthouse in late 1993, my two colleagues and I were anxious to get out and explore this exotic city. At the front gate we were greeted enthusiastically by a group of beaming *cyclo* drivers touting for our business. We selected three at random, settled on an hourly rate, gave them a list of places we wanted to visit and off we went. At times we were three *cyclos* abreast, whirring through the streets towards the Temple of Literature, the Ho Chi Minh Mausoleum and Museum, and assorted pagodas, feeling rather adventurous, and at times terrified, as we weaved in and out of the traffic.

For a city like Hanoi at that time it was an ideal way to sightsee. The speed of a *cyclo* is slow enough for you to take in the sights and you are close to the action so you can hear and smell, and even stop and buy something from a roadside seller without getting out of your seat. It is a better alternative to walking, obviously because it is less strenuous—for you, at least—but also because the pavements are often in poor repair, and are uneven and cluttered with parked bikes, stalls or goods overflowing from shops, so it becomes difficult to look at anything other than where you are putting your feet. Sitting back, relaxing in a *cyclo* means you can look up and be rewarded with the sight of once-beautiful French colonial buildings, some large and grand, others small and quaint with a special detail or ornamentation that catches the eye, and enjoy seemingly limitless vistas along wide tree-lined boulevards, invariably passing parks, lakes and heroic statues on the way.

Nothing was too much trouble for our drivers as they practised their limited English, pointing out sights of interest. Gail was busily photographing everything in sight when we spotted an enormous pig, recently killed and being transported in a *cyclo*, with blood and intestines draining into a bowl. Looking like a scene from a Keystone Cops comedy, there we were, three Western women in three *cyclos* in full chase of this pig in a *cyclo*, laughing hysterically as we spun around corners, worrying that we would have pig's intestines flying all over us if we got any closer, until Gail finally got her shot.

During our ten-day stay we hired these same *cyclo* drivers to do further sightseeing when we had spare time, and to take us to restaurants or the water puppets. On those days when we were busy working and couldn't go out with them, they would be disappointed but nevertheless would give us a friendly greeting. On our final day we had a free morning before leaving for the airport, so we decided to do a last *cyclo* tour for a couple of hours. Just before taking us back to the guesthouse, our drivers stopped and asked us to wait a moment. Left sitting in our *cyclos*, stranded in the gutter, we wondered what was going on. Surely if they needed a toilet break, we discussed, they could have waited another five or ten minutes when we would have finished our trip. Nothing like this had happened on previous outings. And then they appeared, broad smiles and each carrying a bunch of red roses wrapped in cellophane and tied with a ribbon. To wish us luck, they said! We, who were born of a lucky generation in a lucky country, were receiving good wishes and gifts from impoverished *cyclo* drivers in one of the poorest countries on Earth. Of course, the cynic could say we had obviously paid them too much or they were practising good public relations. But the cynic would miss the point that Vietnamese are romantics: friendly, generous and charming. And while commerce is important (literally a matter of life and death for many), it is not what moves their spirit. What language could not express, the flowers could and our three wonderful drivers, who had given their best for us, were waiting at the gate of the hotel when we left for the airport to wave us goodbye and to see us wave their red roses back at them.

After returning to Australia I sent Hung, my *cyclo* driver, some photos we had taken together. Then, unexpectedly, I found that I would be returning to Vietnam in a few weeks on a trade mission. I was staying at a different hotel this trip, but after only half a day, Hung had discovered that I was back in town. An impressive bush telegraph! My tight schedule left time for only a brief visit to the drivers to give them some small souvenirs, but I told them I would be back again in another month. Even though I was staying at yet another hotel on this third trip, Hung was waiting outside as I emerged from checking in. The network was really in good form!

When I returned to Hanoi some months later to live there full-time, Hung arrived at my room with flowers to welcome me and an invitation to visit his home and family. Since then we have shared many experiences. I have visited his home many times and met his parents, brothers and sisters, aunts and uncles, wife and children and friends. We have laughed together many times, and when his second child died after only a few short days of life, we cried together. A year later when his wife gave birth to a beautiful healthy daughter, we could celebrate again, especially grateful for this precious new gift.

Hung's father was in the Army until he retired, as was Hung until 1989 when the Vietnamese Army was drastically downsized. Hung, his wife and now two children lived in one room, a damp cement box without windows in which the hard wooden bed takes up just about the entire floor space. A ladder goes up into a tiny space in the roof, which was sometimes used as a bedroom, but it must have been like an oven in summer. Across an alleyway is some sort of communal cooking place and washing is done at a communal tap. Initially this area developed as a sort of shantytown where people just grabbed a piece of land to live on. Despite the fact that it was outside the city dyke and therefore flooded regularly, it was close to the centre of Hanoi which meant opportunities to eke out a living somehow. These days there are signs of progress and prosperity and the bustle of commercial enterprises in the streets. But when the floods come, everyone has to move out and the high water mark, at about two metres, can be clearly seen on the walls of Hung's room. Hung's parents live nearby in somewhat better circumstances but, even so, their life is not easy or comfortable. Yet despite the wide disparity between our means, it is I who feel I have received more than I could ever give. I have been presented with flowers for my birthday and for Women's Day. Sometimes if Hung was waiting for me, he would buy some bananas from a passing seller to give me. Another time he and his son came to visit and surprised me with a framed print to hang on my wall.

Better than material goods, though, I have been given a small part in Hung's family. I have shared lunch at Tet with his family, and attended the birthday party of his new baby. We went to the Zoo together one Sunday, Hung pedalling me and his son in the *cyclo*, his wife and cousin riding alongside on a pushbike. One night I took the family to a restaurant, probably the first time they had ever been to a proper restaurant and they came all dressed up in their best clothes for the occasion. Another time we all went to the circus in Lenin Park, where Hung was particularly delighted in seeing a monkey pedalling a miniature *cyclo*.

I was away from Hanoi when Hung's five-day-old baby died. When I returned, one of Hung's *cyclo*-driver friends told me about it and the next day Hung came to see me and took me to his home to visit his wife. At times like this you really understand the grinding, relentless, poverty-stricken existence of these people. As we sat in their bitterly cold, damp and dingy room, they showed me the few relics they had to remind them of their lost baby—some chest X-rays, a hospital tag with the baby's name (Hoang), weight (three kilograms) and sex (male), and a prescription and receipt for some medicine costing US$2. What may be merely a slight setback for a baby born in an affluent modern society can be fatal in a country like Vietnam, and there was little comfort for Hung's wife, with her tear-stained face and breasts full with now unneeded milk.

I went to visit again two weeks later and Hung asked me to go with him the following day to the cemetery where the baby had been buried. Of course I agreed, but at first I wasn't sure why it was important to them that I should, until Hung asked me to bring my camera. In the absence of any photos of their baby in life, the best they could record was his death. It took two hours for the round trip, with Hung pedalling fast to keep from freezing in the icy wind that day. At the cemetery we found the maternity hospital section where Hung's baby was buried, an area of tiny clay mounds with a number of freshly dug graves waiting. Obviously the bleak weather, malnutrition, poverty and lack of good health care were exacting a heavy toll that winter. Distinguishing it from most of the other small graves, Hung had erected a tiny stone plaque with his baby's name and the dates of his short life. The photos I took that day could be added to their small collection of memories and join photos of other past family members on their simple family altar in their otherwise bare and cheerless room.

A year later, this same room was the scene of a happy event— a party for Hung's new daughter. For the first month after a birth, mothers and babies stay confined to the home. After that time, family and friends are invited to a birthday party. An impossible number of people were crammed into Hung's tiny room that afternoon and somehow a feast to feed them was prepared. Grannies and aunts (me included), babies and toddlers were packed together to sit on the bed. Children and men sat on the floor, on small stools or spilled out the doorway, leaning on walls. It is amazing what happiness and human fellowship can do. In this case it brought warmth and cheer to these dismal surroundings and no baby, rich or poor, could have had a better welcome and celebration of its new life.

When Hung's mother died, I was summoned to attend a ceremony at Quan Su pagoda, the headquarters of the Buddhist religion in Vietnam. Unlike countries such as Thailand and Laos, where the pagodas and temples seem filled with young male novices in their bright saffron robes, the pagodas in Vietnam are mainly the domain of the old women. This is one of the few outlets open to respectable women, who have come to the end of their working and child-raising lives, where they can find space for quiet contemplation as well as some company as they tend and decorate the pagodas. Dressed in their dull brown robes, their brown wooden beads around their neck, these women sat in front of the friends and family who had gathered for the service for Hung's mother. At the front was the *bonze*, who played the wooden drum and led the chant. The monotonous beat, the chanting, the swirling incense smoke, the flickering shadows among the red and gold statues was hypnotic and soothing—initially at least. But after three hours, my cramped Western legs and numb bottom could take no more. I signalled to Hung and asked how much longer, and my heart slumped when he told me the ceremony would go for some hours more, but then he went on to say that it was acceptable to leave at any time, the important thing was to have come at all. I wished I had known that about two hours earlier!

Over the years, long periods would elapse without me seeing Hung, but I would always try to visit at Tet and take small gifts for the children or clothes for his wife. I was always treated with such enthusiasm and charm whenever I visited, regardless of what they might be doing. Family members would be summoned, cups of tea and fruit prepared, protocols inquiring after the health of my family satisfied. But while the rituals remained constant, the family fortunes seemed extremely unstable.

A year after I had first met Hung he proudly told me he had saved up half the price of a small television. About two years after that he had given up his *cyclo* and bought a motorbike to become a motorbike taxi, or *xe om*, driver, following the current trend in Hanoi. Clearly he saw this as a step up, but I was always puzzled by the pricing policy commonly adopted by all the drivers. *Cyclo* drivers charged more than *xe om* drivers for the same journey, whether the passenger was a foreigner or a local. This didn't seem to make economic sense from either the driver or customer viewpoint. Motorbike travel got you to your destination faster and motorbikes could travel on roads where *cyclos* were now banned, so as a customer you might expect to pay more. From the driver's side, the initial outlay for even the cheapest motorbike was many times that of a *cyclo*, and on top of that there were petrol, oil and maintenance costs. So while the *xe om* driver might use less leg power, and he might fit in more trips, he received less money than a *cyclo* driver for each trip and considerably less profit taking into account the initial outlay and overheads.

Like the Vietnamese economy in general during the period of 1993 to 1996, life seemed to be improving for Hung and his family. His brother, I learned, had a plumbing business and was doing well. His parents were renovating their house, and next they had a telephone connected. Then after a gap of maybe another year, I invited Hung to visit me and he came on a bicycle, explaining that he had had to sell his motorbike to pay the bills. This meant not only loss of transport but loss of his means of income and he was reduced to finding labouring work where he could, not an easy task. More time passed and he had a motorbike again, but some of his friends would tell me he was gambling every day.

There are some things about Vietnam and Vietnamese that foreigners will never understand—like the ups and downs of Hung's family's fortune—except in that general sense that, like the poor everywhere, there is little cushioning from the blows life deals, no nest egg put aside for a rainy day, nothing to fall back on. After his mother died I called by one day and found that Hung and his father were now in the billiard table-making business. The whole front of the house was full of billiard table tops leaning against each other along both side walls. Making small talk as I sipped my tea with them, I discovered that I could buy a full-size table plus cues and a set of balls, all for US$55. Suddenly owning a billiard table seemed like the thing to do. After a quick check back home to see if it would fit, my table was delivered, and Hung and his friends christened it with a game after installation. The table looked terrific—just like the real thing. But like many things Vietnamese, appearance isn't everything. It took some special skills both to 'read' the surface of the table (as the humidity of Hanoi warped the wooden base) and to squeeze the balls past the non-standard openings.

About a year later I went to Hung's father's house with some friends who wanted to purchase their own billiard table, only to find they were now out of the billiard table business. Instead of billiard tabletops lining the walls, shelving had been installed and was laden with long lengths of PVC piping and plumbing fittings. This latest enterprise seemed to be success-ful, and certainly everyone appeared very happy about it. After his wife's death, Hung's father looked very old and ill. When I mentioned this to Hung he agreed and told me he thought his father would probably die within six months. But the plumb-ing business gave him a new lease on life, it seemed. He looked fit and active and was clearly happy to be involved, even though he had lost most of his living room.

When I packed up to leave Hanoi for good in 2002, I went to Hung's house to say a final farewell. His father was looking younger and stronger than ever and was so proud and happy to tell me he had been able to buy a small house nearby for Hung and insisted I inspect it. But the gods always send mixed bless-ings it seems, for Hung and his wife were now divorced and Hung's son had dropped out of school and was in danger of getting into trouble.

Hung's story can be seen as a microcosm of the changes that affected the whole country. Doors opened and foreigners entered, bringing new opportunities for prosperity but also many other social changes, some positive, some negative. The learning curve was, and is, steep. The rate of change is so fast. Changes that I have witnessed over half a century in Australia I saw occur in less than a decade in Vietnam. Hung's family and I shared only a small number of words and I was ignorant of many of their ways and customs, and also of their real situation and how to help. We were worlds apart in almost every way. But I do know that although life was always hard, they were always cheerful, always played the gracious host, and let me share a small part of their life.

Matchmaking

It is hard for Vietnamese to ever be alone. Vietnam is one of the most densely populated countries in the world, and added to that are the cultural norms and economic imperatives that result in two or three generations of extended families living together in close proximity. An Australian couple living and working in Hanoi decided they needed to get out of the city and have a weekend away. They told their staff that they wanted to get away and be alone. 'What a good idea,' replied the office manager. 'We'll come too and we can all be alone together!'

Being unmarried and/or childless is considered a sad state of affairs by Vietnamese. Travelling alone by choice or, even worse, living in a foreign country alone is tragic and incomprehensible to them. And so my language teacher Mrs Thanh, who had already introduced me to Hanoi's fortune tellers, and her friend Mrs Thu saw it as their duty—as well as their pleasure, I am sure—to try to find me a suitable boyfriend or perhaps even a husband.

Their first effort was Mr Tam. Mrs Thu had friends who had apparently made their reputations as successful matchmakers. I didn't know this when I was taken to visit them, otherwise I would have been more cautious about joining in what I thought was innocent banter about boyfriends and marriage, dismissing as fantasy their claim to have a friend who spoke excellent English, was very handsome and was very interested in acquiring a foreign wife. A few days later I was stunned to learn that a meeting had been set up by the matchmakers, with them even taking time off work to be there to support their candidate, Mr Tam. There was no way I could escape this ordeal without causing Mrs Thu and her friends to lose face.

The dreaded day arrived and I was collected by Mrs Thanh and Mrs Thu, who remained on either side of me throughout the whole embarrassing procedure. I was instructed by them to lie about my age, subtracting two years so he was an ideal seven years older. When I suggested that this might not be a good basis for starting a relationship, Mrs Thu dismissed my concerns, saying of course it was alright to lie about such matters and that she had certainly done so to catch her young husband. It was an extremely uncomfortable two hours as I tried to be pleasant but not give any encouragement or make matters worse. Mr Tam, however, was clearly in his element as he tried to impress me with his learning, mentioning nonchalantly that he had read Shakespeare in both English and Russian, and telling me about his business and his new process for the extraction of gold, and how rich this would make him.

The following week my parents arrived in Hanoi to visit me, and my friends announced that Mr Tam would come to meet them. By this time it was clear I had lost control of the situation and short of creating a scene, I had no alternative but to agree. But I limited the visit to thirty minutes, claiming my parents' packed itinerary as the excuse. Then I had to try to explain, rather sheepishly, this bizarre situation to my elderly parents, who were already suffering some culture shock on their first visit to Vietnam. Right on time the delegation arrived— Mr Tam and his matchmaker friend, both dressed in suits, accompanied by Mrs Thanh and Mrs Thu. And for thirty minutes Mr Tam proceeded to impress my bewildered parents, first demonstrating his learning and education, then telling them about his business, and to lend some veracity to his claims, showing them a small speck of gold stuck on a piece of paper. Eventually we made our escape, pleading a dinner engagement. Not having any experience in such a situation, my parents had played a passive role in the proceedings, waiting to see what would happen next. I was anxious about their reaction and hurriedly reassured them that my friends now understood from me that this was to go no further, so I was completely taken aback when my mother said she thought he was okay and that she had always fancied a mouthful of gold teeth! For a moment I had a vision of her selling me off to Mr Tam and smiling an 18-carat smile all the way back to Australia.

After this fiasco I tried to explain to Mrs Thanh that I was really happy in my single and alone state and, what's more, I had many friends and many opportunities, if I wanted, to find my own partner. Fixing me with a 'glittering eye' as I imagined from the Ancient Mariner, she replied triumphantly, as she glanced meaningfully at my bed, 'Of course you have many friends—but no result!' According to her, I only had 'a short time left to love', since fifty years of age was the cut-off point, she believed—although later, as my fifty came and went, she gave Westerners a few extra years of grace. Another time she told me that her government had introduced an 'open door' policy and that maybe I should do the same!

My favourite Mrs Thanh story concerns her woman friend, who despite being married had had a lover for many years. Over the years the couple had few opportunities to be together, maybe only once a year. These meetings were fraught with danger and were extraordinarily complicated. Once they planned to spend a night together, but to avoid being recognised they travelled almost one hundred kilometres from Hanoi, which by motorbike on the poor roads could mean three or four hours' riding. The woman told her family she was staying with a family friend for the night. She was unable to leave Hanoi safely until after 9pm to avoid being recognised on the roads, and of course, she would have to be back very early the next morning ready to start work at 7.30am. This seemed not only a dangerous plan, but exhausting, too. But it was nothing compared to the escapade they concocted the following year.

The plan was for this woman to fly to Ho Chi Minh City for the night, since her lover had to be there for business. Her cover story was that she was going to another province with Mrs Thanh to visit her relatives. Mrs Thanh went to the travel agent to purchase the plane ticket to reduce the danger of her friend being recognised, and even lent her some money. Then Mrs Thanh had to lock herself in her apartment all weekend to avoid being found out in this deceit. When she found she unexpectedly needed to go out, she had to disguise herself with a hat, scarf and dark glasses, since she was supposed to be in the provinces with her friend.

As it turned out, the plan came unstuck and everyone involved had a seriously worrying time. Mrs Thanh came to see me at the end of the drama, looking terrible after a sleepless night. The lovers had met in Ho Chi Minh City, but when they tried to confirm the flight back to Hanoi, they found they didn't have seats. The woman rang Mrs Thanh, who told her to go back and stay at the airline office for as long as it took, and to pay whatever amount of money was required—as long as she got back to Hanoi! Ultimately she succeeded and her husband was none the wiser, but no doubt she and Mrs Thanh aged considerably that weekend. I thought the moral of the story was going to be that this couple should carefully reconsider any future exploits or at least plan more carefully, taking account of possible contingencies. But Mrs Thanh extracted quite a different lesson from the story for me. She pointed out that the year before had involved her friend travelling maybe two hundred kilometres and paying a small amount of money. This year, she had to travel even further, about three thousand kilometres, and pay a couple of hundred US dollars. So her warning to me was that if I waited much longer for such adventures, I wouldn't be able to travel the distance or afford the money needed!

Almost two years after the Mr 'gold nuggets' Tam affair, I went to visit Mrs Thu to pay my respects on the death of her father. However, even in the midst of death, apparently there is still matchmaking to be done. I had been told that I should take fruit and incense, say some prayers before the family altar and leave after about thirty minutes. Mrs Thu had other ideas and, keeping me busy looking at photographs of the funeral, she got busy trying to contact her friend Mr Manh. When she couldn't reach him by phone she drove around to his house to leave a message, and then insisted I wait and have lunch with her. At about 1pm Mr Manh arrived in response to her summons and I was sent back to his place with him to meet his children. He turned out to be a very nice shy man, a university professor in Hanoi who had studied in Bulgaria, and who was left to raise his two sons alone after his wife committed suicide. His children were sweet, and we struggled to make conversation with their limited English and my even more limited Vietnamese until I could decently take my leave.

Despite my warnings to Mrs Thanh and Mrs Thu about any more matchmaking, and telling them that Mr Manh was not the man of my dreams, they went ahead and devised a plan to have lunch at Mr Manh's house one day, with them coming along to do the cooking. When I protested, Mrs Thanh said it was to make his children happy and so I had to agree. And we did have a nice time. Afterwards, Mr Manh told Mrs Thu that he was 'like a cat that had been hungry for a very long time, who suddenly looks up and sees three pieces of meat'! Hardly a comment that would endear him to the sisterhood, but clearly he was happy to have had three woman in his house for a short time.

Over the years, Mrs Thanh continued to take an active interest in my life. Sometimes it was advice on what to wear; according to her I should wear a red skirt and jacket with a white shirt, since it makes me look younger and Vietnamese like red. Another time she complained that I always travelled to other Asian countries for holidays, which according to her were all the same, when I should go to Russia, especially to Moscow and St Petersburg where I would surely find a man to fall in love with, since in her experience it had happened to many Vietnamese who went there. At one stage she was planning to buy a very small motorbike—a Charly, which required you to pedal really fast to get the motor started—so she could take me adventuring. 'Two old ladies on a very small bike,' she would laugh. And she never missed an opportunity to widen my circle of potential partners.

Once it was the dean of her university department whom she tricked me into meeting. After I made my escape and got back to my room, the phone rang and all I heard on the other end was Mrs Thanh laughing. Alexander, her Russian friend who regularly came to Hanoi from Vladivostok to study Vietnamese linguistics and who had introduced me to Mrs Thanh, was always raised as a possibility. 'But he's married!' I would protest. 'Now he is separated,' Mrs Thanh eagerly reported to me when Alexander returned to Hanoi after six months back in Russia. 'I'm not interested!' I cried, but never managed to convince her. I don't know what stories she told him. She once told a group of Vietnamese, while we were at the fortune teller's house, that I had been Miss Australia when I was young, so I knew she was capable of saying anything.

One evening Alexander arrived at my room with a bunch of red roses. On his next trip back to Hanoi, Mrs Thanh brought him to visit me, and with a flourish he flung a long string of pearls around my neck. 'From Russia,' he said proudly. The fact that they were plastic and probably made in China—and maybe even bought at the market in Hanoi under Mrs Thanh's guidance— did not detract from the gesture. When it seemed that Alexander wouldn't be returning to Hanoi again, I was pressured by Mrs Thanh to go to the airport to farewell him, but was actually laid low on the day by a nasty virus. Mrs Thanh couldn't wait to reprimand me, telling me that he had tears in his eyes when told I wasn't coming. In the long run it all turned out for the best— I never had time to take up his invitation to visit Vladivostok and teach a semester at the Far Eastern State Technical University. And a couple of years later when he was back in Hanoi briefly to attend a conference, the three of us met and he told us he was back with his wife and daughter again. A happy ending, but not the one Mrs Thanh had hoped for.

Another of Mrs Thanh's schemes involved an excursion to Tam Dao mountain, about eighty kilometres from Hanoi. There were eight of us travelling on four motorbikes, including Mr Lan whose house we were going to stay in overnight, Mr Kim who was to drive me, and then another group travelling there by minibus. After a ride of about three hours we had to walk the last part along a track and across a stream to reach the beautiful traditional wooden stilt house Mr Lan had bought and moved to this location. Our bathroom was the stream, the toilet just a screened-off area in the bush nearby, and we slept on mats on the floor, women in one room, men in the other. I settled myself in a spot in the corner, not realising that in the packed room, as my room-mates rolled over during the night, I would end up with my nose squashed against the wall. What with the discomfort of being wedged in, the snoring and wild animal noises, I didn't get much sleep, but the hard wooden floor probably helped my back recover after the long ride there.

At 6.30 the next morning we set off to climb the mountain to visit the pagoda at the top. I seemed to be the only foreigner around and as a result I was touched and talked about, hugged and photographed non-stop. The climb was exhausting and the trip downhill just as bad since it was steep, muddy and slippery. Mrs Thanh organised Mr Lan to drive me back to Hanoi, a wonderful trip through the late afternoon shadows, speeding past mother hens and geese gathering their chicks, past pigs and piglets digging in the roadside dirt, and past an endless parade of workers wending their way home after another day of toil much harder than mine. Motorbike travel offers speed and some comfort but with the sensation of closeness to the environment you get from walking. In an air-conditioned vehicle, insulated behind glass, you don't get to experience the smells or the reality of the scenes passed. But on a motorbike, as you pass small villages, you can see the expressions on faces, you can see into their homes and you can see the strain of the labour of the workers in the fields, the mud-caked calloused feet, the material poverty. Despite aching legs for some days after, Mrs Thanh pronounced the excursion a success, especially as she told me that Mr Kim sent me his regards and wanted to invite me dancing.

Before she left Hanoi to work at the University of Malaysia in Kuala Lumpur, Mrs Thanh was determined to organise my life according to her plan. She insisted on taking me to the Saturday afternoon dancing hall run by Mr Dzung. She brought along her English–Vietnamese dictionary and her contract for Kuala Lumpur and continued to work on translating it while I, like an idiot spinster daughter, was told to enjoy myself dancing. Later I noticed her having a private conversation with Mr Dien, whom she thought would be a suitable partner for me, and Mr Dzung the teacher, telling him to look after me and help me learn to dance.

After Mrs Thanh left Hanoi, her best friend Mrs Thu tried to take over responsibility for my love life. She would invite me to her house whenever she held a party for her students who were studying Vietnamese in the hope that one might satisfy me. But I think by this stage her heart was no longer in this quest for a husband. It had become a form of innocent fun and she would tease me relentlessly, including hilarious sentences in our language lessons, using the words 'beside', 'under' and 'on top of', and telling me that Mr Tam and Mr Manh were always ringing her to talk about me.

In many ways these intelligent, well-educated, strong Hanoi women envied me my freedom, but they couldn't quite rid themselves of the traditional idea that a woman's life wasn't complete without a husband. 'It's different for foreigners,' they would reassure each other. I wonder ...

When people asked me why I enjoyed living in Hanoi, I would jokingly reply that 'the food is good and cheap, the clothes fit me, and the men don't care how old I am!' Add to that friends like Mrs Thanh and Mrs Thu, and who needs the Internet and dating services?

Sharing an umbrella
on National Day

It was Vietnamese National Day, 2 September 1995, marking the fiftieth anniversary of that day when Ho Chi Minh first read the Vietnamese Declaration of Independence, and I was standing in a huge crowd at Hoan Kiem Lake, waiting for the fireworks display to begin. Early that morning there had been a grand parade held in Ba Dinh Square in front of the Ho Chi Minh Mausoleum, where an embalmed Uncle Ho, as he is affectionately known, lies in state. The city was bedecked with the red and gold of the national flag, and everywhere people were enjoying the national holiday.

Ho Chi Minh didn't live to see Vietnam's independence—he died in 1969, on National Day, a fact that was initially concealed in case it was interpreted as a bad omen. And there were still many years of war and struggle after 1945, and even after the end of the Vietnam War (or the American War, as the Vietnamese know it), there followed another decade of extreme hardship. But by 1995 it seemed that the light at the end of the tunnel could be seen. The 'open door' policy announced in 1986 appeared to be working, and foreigners were lining up to invest in this small, emerging Asian tiger, bringing much-needed foreign currency, technology and trade.

I had bought a T-shirt to wear for the occasion, red with a large gold star on it like the flag, and after dinner I walked to Hoan Kiem Lake with thousands of others, promenading around the edge of the lake, enjoying the musical performances presented on makeshift stages, and the coloured lights and decorations. All roads in the vicinity were closed to traffic and the streets and adjacent parks quickly filled with people. I had never been in such a huge crowd before and yet it was a wonderful, relaxed atmosphere with no annoying or antisocial behaviour to spoil the festive mood. After one slow circuit of the lake I selected a vantage point among the crowd for watching the fireworks, and it didn't take long for someone to start a conversation with me and others to shyly join in. But there was nothing shy about my new companions when a shower of rain began.

I had come prepared for the capricious weather of Hanoi, but as soon as I opened my umbrella, suddenly there were seven people squeezed up against me, sheltering under it! Fortunately, the shower didn't last long and my conversation with a young man and his eight-year-old daughter continued in this intimate setting. He told me he had only returned to Hanoi a few months before, after six years in a refugee camp in Hong Kong. He told about the tear gas attacks and the beatings by the police in the camps, and about how the children were terrified and had been burnt by the tear gas. Amazingly, there was no bitterness when he spoke of those six years of horror, nor of the circumstances that led to his fleeing his country in the first place. Instead, he spoke optimistically of the future. He had taken advantage of a UN repatriation offer, and with the US$2000 he received for himself, his wife and two children, plus a loan of another US$2000 from a friend, he returned to Hanoi, bought a second-hand car and began a tourist service. He hoped to be able to repay the loan soon from the US$300 per month he could earn this way. He even wrote to his friends back in the camp, telling them they should also return to Hanoi for the sake of their children now that things had changed.

This conversation passed the time while waiting for the fireworks to begin at 9pm. Everyone was waiting so quietly and patiently, not needing anything other than the expectation of the display to come and the sense of being alive, and together and independent at last. Once the fireworks began there were thousands and thousands of expectant and happy faces, old and young, turned skyward, captivated and enjoying the moment. My new friend's little girl was frightened by the noise at first—she thought it was tear gas and gunfire like in the camp—but she was quickly soothed and forgot old fears, and was soon lost in the wonder of it all. Compared to the lavish fireworks displays we have become used to in rich countries, complete with musical accompaniment and gimmicks, I guess it wasn't much of a show. There were thirty minutes of colourful skyrockets in Hanoi, the country's captial, and only twenty minutes in Ho Chi Minh City and Da Nang, this differentiation itself a characteristic display of political one-upmanship and a subtle reminder of where power lies. But the quiet appreciation and happiness of the crowd more than made up for any lack of sophistication.

Vietnamese truly appreciate the fact of being independent, of no longer having war tear their lives apart, of being able to enjoy the simple pleasures of family and community, and having hope for their children's future—things so often taken for granted in 'lucky' countries like Australia. Hanoians say it always rains on National Day, because even the sky cried when Uncle Ho died. But I think Uncle Ho would have been happy on that fiftieth anniversary, twenty-six years after his death, to see the start of a new era of hope and happiness. And the rain brought me a story of optimism and courage under my umbrella.

Talking about jazz is talking about Minh

At the end of the day, the fruit and vegetable sellers, with their conical hats and shoulder poles, slowly make their way home along the motorbike-clogged streets. The street vendors hook up their lights and arrange their tables and stools, ready for the evening trade. As you pick your way through the throngs of playing children, scampering dogs and families sitting on the pavements enjoying the night air, there, above the roar of the traffic, the honking of horns, the cries of food sellers, you can hear traditional Vietnamese melodies coming from open doors and windows. Sometimes from a nearby karaoke bar the strains of the latest popular song are caught hanging in the air. But after 1997 there was a new and maybe unexpected sound in the air in Hanoi: the sound of Minh's hot sax playing modern jazz.

If you went inside Minh's new jazz club, you could be forgiven for thinking you had left Asia completely and, judging by the sophisticated Western ambience of the place, were instead inside a club in Europe or the United States. This would be all the more surprising when you learnt that until the year before, in 1996, Minh had never been outside Vietnam, let alone inside a jazz club. But this only serves to highlight the remarkable journey of a man possessed by a passion for jazz, who has for more than thirty years pursued his dream of bringing an understanding and love of jazz to his country.

Playing with the radio dial one day in 1968 looking for music, a teenage Minh first heard Benny Goodman on Voice of America radio. 'Benny Goodman got in here and here,' says Minh, pointing to his heart and his head. From that moment on, Minh knew he wanted to play music like that.

Minh's whole family is musical. His father played saxophone and guitar, but only as an amateur, having to support his family by other means. All Minh's siblings play instruments—clarinet, guitar, cello—and now Minh's children keep the family tradition going. But it was Minh's mother, a well-known professional singer of traditional Vietnamese songs with Vietnam Radio in Hanoi, who probably exerted the greatest influence on the young Minh. Following the rapture of discovery, Minh quickly realised that if he wanted to play jazz, it was going to be a lonely journey with no-one to guide him.

Jazz was unknown in Vietnam then; there were no books, music, records or tapes available, and anyway, such things were out of the reach of people struggling to survive and cut off from most of the world. But his mother gave him hope and encouragement and bought him a clarinet. 'If you really want to learn how to play jazz,' she told him, 'you just need to listen and teach yourself.' And that is exactly what he did, locked away in his room, his ear to the radio long into the night, scanning the airways in the hope of catching that elusive sound that touched his soul, dreaming of playing like Benny Goodman, and escaping for a time from the harsh reality of his war-torn country.

Then came 1986, the year of *doi moi*, Vietnam's economic renovation—its new 'open door' policy. The ramifications of this policy extended well beyond governments and trade to touch the lives of ordinary people, opening up new worlds and new opportunities for them. That year, Minh met a foreigner from the UK who had come to work in Vietnam and who played jazz as a hobby. For the first time, Minh had someone who understood him and could supply him with some sheet music and tapes to satisfy his hunger.

Just a couple of years later, Minh gave his first jazz concert in Vietnam where he played 'In the Mood', 'Danny Boy' and 'Stardust'. 'Ah, "Stardust" is wonderful for sax,' he says with feeling. However, the problem with being a pioneer was that there was no local audience who could appreciate jazz, no-one who could understand improvisation, and no place to play. As more foreigners came to live in Vietnam, Minh found a small but appreciative audience, and in 1991 he formed his first quartet, consisting of bass, clarinet, synthesiser and saxophone, to play at a function at the French embassy in Hanoi. Since that time, the number of foreigners coming to Hanoi has increased, and Minh and his various groups, including his teenage son, have played in many popular venues around town—the Metropole, the Stone Elephant, the Sunset Pub, Gustave's, the American club, and at private parties. Then, on 5 September 1997, Minh, achieving the once unimaginable, opened his own jazz club in Hanoi. Finally he had a place to play the music he loves, just the way he wanted.

That year was a big year for Minh in other ways, too. He was appointed to teach at the Hanoi School of Music and opened the first course in jazz studies at the Hanoi Conservatorium. Earlier in the year he was honoured by the then President of Vietnam, Le Duc Anh, and presented with the award of Eminent Artist in a ceremony held at the Ho Chi Minh Museum in Hanoi, the only saxophonist to be recognised this way in Vietnam. You can see this award hanging in Minh's club, although it is somewhat overshadowed by pictures of his heroes covering the walls—those legends of jazz Coltrane, Getz, Parker, Goodman and Brubeck—which is just as Minh likes it.

It has been a long and arduous trailblazing journey for Minh, yet he remains as passionate as ever about his music. 'Jazz music is my life,' he says simply. Even when playing classical music, Minh is still thinking jazz. The first time the saxophone was played publicly in Vietnam was by Minh, at a concert at Hanoi's Opera House in 1988, where he played Bach, Mozart and Haydn. He played there again in 1989 and 1994. And he likes to tell, with a twinkle in his eyes, how he would always try to inject a jazz note somehow, even in the classical pieces he was playing. 'People wouldn't know what they were hearing,' he explained, 'but they knew it was something different and they liked it.'

Despite the public recognition Minh has recently received, and the realisation of his dream of having his own jazz club, Minh is not ready to rest on his laurels. He sees that he still has much to do. Over the years, the proportion of Vietnamese in his audience has been gradually increasing, but still the knowledge of jazz is not widespread. Minh hopes, now that he has his own club, to hold jazz appreciation sessions for young people, where he can share his love and knowledge and help them understand the music. Deprived of any music and guidance himself when young, he understands only too well what it is like to be hungry for knowledge, and sees an opportunity now to share the richness of his experience, his books, his tapes and discs, and most of all, his passion. He has great hopes for his son, too, who has all the advantages Minh lacked at his age. But while justly proud of his son's ability, he sees to it that he keeps his feet firmly on the ground, demanding discipline and dedication, and letting him know he still has a lot of maturing to do.

It is impossible not to be affected by Minh's passion and obsession with music, and there is no doubt he will be remembered as a significant figure in the history of jazz in Vietnam. Minh may be considered the 'grand old man of jazz' in his country, but his sparkle and energy is that of a young man with a vision of bringing jazz to everyone. He is modest and more hesitant to speak about his personal ambition, which is to develop a distinctive Vietnamese jazz. 'Vietnamese traditional music has a lot of rhythm and melody,' Minh explains, 'so is very suitable for jazz.' So far he has written six of his own jazz compositions, blending traditional Vietnamese music from the Centre, the Highlands, the South and North regions of Vietnam with a modern jazz style. The result is an interesting, and at times quite haunting blend of East and West. But then, this is a country with a long history of soaking up influences from both East and West and turning them into something distinctively Vietnamese. Thankfully, these days the invasions are peaceful, with French tourists or American expatriates vying for a chance to play a gig with Minh's group.

Minh remains faithful to his boyhood dream and is still inspired by his heroes. He dreams of going to New Orleans one day, too. And as the new century begins, it seems likely that he will inspire the genesis of a distinctive Vietnamese jazz and succeed in leading a new generation of young talented musicians to a place in the world of jazz.

Cops and robbers

After eighteen months of trouble-free living in Vietnam, I was completely lulled into feeling safe and secure at all times. Protected by guesthouse staff, minded well by my friends, and not being inclined to visit potential trouble spots, I was beginning to believe there was no crime in Hanoi. And so, with an unguarded attitude, I strolled across the street near my guesthouse one Sunday evening just after 7pm and was staggered to find myself the victim of a bag snatching. Two young men on a motorbike drove slowly behind me just as I was about to step onto the footpath, pulled my bag from my shoulder and drove away. No sound was made—certainly not by me because I was too stunned to even shout. Not that yelling would have achieved much by the time my slow wits registered the theft, and by then the thieves were well on their way, swallowed up by the swirling current of motorbikes, bicycles, cars and *cyclos*. Then, as if to make up for the slow-motion, dream-like nature of the theft itself, everything seemed to speed up and in no time I found myself surrounded by Vietnamese friends at the local police station for what was to be the beginning of a somewhat Kafkaesque experience.

As fate would have it, I hadn't cleaned out my bag from a recent trip, so it contained all that was precious and vital to me: passport and visa, credit cards, driver's licence, as well as money, address book, favourite lipstick and other personal items. It took a couple of hours to supply the police with all the required information. Passport and visa details were given, along with a complete list of items stolen (even to the detail of the denomination of currency) and the events described minutely—all in two languages. I was not very enthusiastic since it seemed like a waste of time. There seemed no likelihood of ever catching the thieves, no chance of having my things returned, and so my mind was already racing ahead, planning how to go about replacing the essentials.

However, my Vietnamese friends were all being very encouraging, reassuring me that the thieves would be caught and my belongings returned. How naive they are, I thought! I was a knowing veteran, a victim of several robberies at home in Australia and abroad, with a cynical attitude about the limits of a police force. 'Claim it on insurance, luv,' was the best I could get in Australia, despite fingerprints and in one case a description of the thief. In Germany, I had my handbag 'picked' on Hamburg railway station while waiting for a train to Berlin. Again there was that feeling of disbelief as I searched for my train ticket, increasing to panic when I realised I was on a train with no ticket, no money, no passport, no traveller's cheques, no credit card and no contact details for the friend I was to visit in Berlin. Of course, I dutifully reported the incident to the Berlin authorities, but as I had known, it was to no avail— just another case of claiming on insurance when and if I ever got back to Australia.

Armed with this experience, I quickly dismissed any possibility of ever seeing my snatched bag and its contents again, and over the next couple of weeks set about replacing my belongings. The first priority was my passport, and that was reasonably straightforward since I had a photocopy of the stolen one and was quite well known at the Australian embassy. Within about ten days I had a new passport. The only annoying thing was that my old passport had contained, unusually, a reasonably flattering photo; at least, it was one I would have been happy enough to live with for another few years, whereas now I had to have a photo taken when I had a severe head cold and blocked sinuses, which no amount of steam inhalation or medication could help. So much for vanity!

I knew that replacing my passport was only the prelude, the first tiny step in the journey to replace my Vietnamese visa. And this is where I began to feel like a character in a Kakfa novel. The routine went something like this. In order to get a new visa I needed a copy of the police report of the theft. However, the police would not provide a copy—I suspected it was because they couldn't find (or hadn't kept) the report, since there were certainly no visible signs of a system which efficiently recorded and could retrieve information. But my friends told me this was quite normal and we just had to find the way to get the report out of them. So then I sought an agreement that if I wrote out what I had already reported to the police and then got the police to stamp and sign it as true and accurate, the visa office would accept that as a *de facto* police report.

The stumbling block with this solution was that I had written my account in English whereas what was required was a Vietnamese version, so I was directed by the police to a special government translating verification service across the road. Unfortunately, it was closed that day. Later, my friends told me

I may have to wait in this office two days or more—actually sit all day in the office, waiting my turn. So they suggested an alternative strategy which involved going back to the police to see if they would sign and verify an unofficial Vietnamese version, which my friends would prepare and which I would sign as true and accurate, and which the police could then read. This prompted much discussion and consideration by the police but was finally rejected. My friends remained indefatigable, and eventually, after weeks of visits and discussions with the police, an agreement was reached. Miss Chi, the guesthouse receptionist, who was known to them to be of good and reliable character, translated my written report into Vietnamese, and after some more days and much time spent waiting in offices, I finally had in my hand a verified copy of the police report to take to the visa office.

This was to prove only a trial run, however, for the much more cumbersome and even less helpful bureaucracy surrounding immigration and visa procedures. In the end, Miss Chi and I had to acknowledge defeat; we were sent from office to office, location to location, and then back again, never finding the right person who could deal with this problem. Just as it was looking like we would never sort things out, we ran into someone we knew whose job, it turned out, was to arrange visas and who took pity on me and took things in hand. Then I waited another ten days with some trepidation to see how long my new visa would be for, since it can be a lottery at times, ranging from three months to one or two years. Thankfully, all went well and my original expiry date was restored.

By now, more than a month had passed and all thoughts of the actual theft had been put aside. My bruised arm and wrist were better; I had my new passport, visa, even my new credit card had arrived, and I was busy at work. Then one day, I had a visit from the police, who told the guesthouse manager that they had caught the thieves and recovered my belongings. Two days after that visit I was summoned to a police station and, after a morning of red tape, was handed my old passport and visa, old credit card, Australian driver's licence and an old phone card with about fifty cents' credit left on it. There was no mention of the bag or any other contents, except they did say the thieves had admitted to taking my umbrella too, but threw it away as it was too old and dilapidated. In the course of our conversation, the police also said I would eventually get my US$250 back.

I had to admit at that point that I had been wrong, and it was not my friends but me who was naive. I now understood that in a society like Vietnam, where the police are ubiquitous, nothing goes undetected. Where people live so close together there is little privacy, and where poverty is the norm, any unusual expenditure is very noticeable. I was impressed that the police had caught those responsible and recovered some of my belongings, even though I had replaced all of them by now. But I couldn't believe I would ever see the cash again.

In Vietnam, optimism seems to be the prevailing philosophy; where Westerners would most likely respond with a definite 'no', Vietnamese are more inclined to say 'not yet'. If you ask if someone is married, they never reply 'no', it is always 'not yet'. Ask an old woman if she has a family and she will say 'not yet', regardless of the likelihood. When my friends persisted in asking if my stolen money had been returned yet, I told them I had no expectation that it would ever be returned. They would gently correct me, saying that of course it would be returned to me, and indeed, it was only a matter of time—about another two weeks, in fact. And it was done in an unpredictable and uniquely Vietnamese way.

A note was delivered to the guesthouse and Miss Chi informed me that my presence was expected at the police station that afternoon. Apparently this was a summons to be obeyed, so I had to do a lot of shuffling of appointments. After lunch I set off with one of the young women who worked at the guesthouse to help me with interpretation. We found the policeman who had returned my other belongings and were told to wait while he went off to change into his uniform. He returned with a colleague, and after some milling about where no-one seemed to know what to do next, I was invited to ride behind him on his motorbike to Hanoi's main police station, at Hoan Kiem Lake. We arrived to a scene of great activity, with dozens of police officers and cameras and videos, and were ushered into a meeting room with a large central table, where we were offered tea by a charming uniformed interpreter whose excellent English had a trace of a southern American accent. I was stunned to find that this was going to be a public ceremony staged to return my stolen cash. I was introduced to the head of Hanoi police, the head of the Hoan Kiem police station, and then with cameras rolling the money was dutifully counted out and handed over to me. Speeches were made, and I even had the opportunity to say some words about the diligence of the police department. Great attention had been paid to detail, and my money was returned in exactly the same currency and denominations as I had reported.

Outside, after the formal ceremony, I had some photos taken with some of the police and then made my way home, feeling a little like I had won a lottery prize and beauty contest. No doubt this was an orchestrated piece of public relations, providing a story and some pictures for both the local press and the security program on local television, boosting public confidence in the police force and showing the government crackdown on crime to be working. But that did not detract from the fact that the culprits were caught and property restored, all in a most unexpected and stylish manner.

I thought this would be the end of the matter, and apart from writing a letter of praise to the local paper thanking the police, I put all thoughts of the incident out of my mind. Then early in 1996 I had a visit from the policeman in charge of the case, asking me to write out yet another account of the theft, as he was preparing papers for the court case. Another six months passed before I received a notice from the Hanoi People's Committee requiring my attendance at court. Rachel, a friend and fellow victim of the same thieves, was also called to attend. Apparently we were their only victims still living in Hanoi.

As we waited for the court to open, a police van pulled up outside the courthouse gate. A crowd of people who had been quietly waiting outside gathered around it; they were the family and friends of the two accused young men. Just before 9am we were ushered inside the courtroom where the two culprits, dressed in faded blue prison pyjamas and handcuffed together, were now seated on a bench facing the front of the room. Rachel and I were told to sit in the front row of the public section of the courtroom, and behind us sat the two families. On the other side of the room sat a large number of young people, no doubt friends and fellow students of the accused.

We had assumed that since we were required to appear, an interpreter would be provided by the court. However, it turned out that no-one was available. A young woman who worked there made a valiant effort to explain this to us in English, but she was inadequate for the task of interpreter for the full proceedings. We were invited into a small room which turned out to be the judge's chambers, and some discussions were held about this language problem. The judge explained that since I had already had my stolen goods returned, it was not essential that I stay for the hearing, although I was welcome to do so. But since Rachel had not yet been compensated, they believed it was important that she stay and understand the proceedings and the process of restitution. The large sum of money stolen from her had been used by the thieves to purchase a motorbike, and since this motorbike was now considered an 'instrument of the crime' it had been confiscated by the State and could therefore not be sold to compensate her loss. This hearing, they explained to her, was an opportunity for her to voice her opinion and offer any suggestions to the court. Without an adequate interpreter this would not be possible, so it was decided another date should be set for the hearing. The Vietnamese officials didn't seem too worried about this problem, but Rachel and I were concerned, imagining the anguish of the thieves and their families if it was called off, knowing they would have to wait in limbo for another date to be set and then go through it all again just because we couldn't understand the language. Rachel asked to use a phone and through her network of contacts managed in a very short time to get us a delightful young man, Minh, who was a solicitor working in a law firm, to act as our interpreter.

Now that the proceedings could get under way, everyone took their places. Behind the bench were three enormous baronial-style chairs which dwarfed their occupants. In the middle sat the chairperson of the judging committee, with the two members of the committee on either side of her. To one side, and at a right angle to the bench, sat the court reporter, who, with no machine to lighten the load, recorded the proceedings. On the other side of the room, opposite her, sat a uniformed man whom Minh told us was from the Organs of Control office. Apparently this is part of the police and security forces, but to our ears it sounded more like a comic-book superhero organisation. Next to the Organs of Control representative, and nearest the prisoners, sat a policeman who kept falling asleep during the proceedings, when he wasn't reading his newspaper or going outside to enjoy a cigarette with several other uniformed men who were lounging about. But the finishing touch to the scene was provided by a Vietnamese version of Charles Dickens's French Revolution character, Madam Defarge. Sitting under a clock with its hands permanently stuck on 7.45 was an old woman, not seemingly connected to anyone in the room, busily sewing a bright pink satin pillowcase. Towards the end of the proceedings she must have been feeling a bit tired because she packed away her sewing and went to the back of the room to lie down on one of the benches for a nap.

The two accused had no defence lawyer, and since they had been caught red-handed and admitted guilt, the hearing was to determine punishment. The leading judge began questioning first one and then the other, establishing the facts and trying to ascertain who was the leader, who had planned the robberies, what their motives were, what they had done with the stolen goods and so on. The culprits were medical students at university, aged twenty and twenty-one years. They had allegedly used the stolen money to purchase a motorbike and gold jewellery, and to entertain their friends. The father of each boy was called to the front of the court to answer questions about the family's role, what they had thought when they saw their sons with these items, and what their sons had told them.

The second judge was quite an old man and he directed a great deal of anger towards the boys. In a lengthy tirade, he told them that not only had they broken the trust placed upon them by their parents and brought dishonour to their families, but by robbing foreigners they had shamed Vietnam.

Foreigners come to Vietnam to do business and to assist in the economic development of the country, he told them, but because of such robberies, they became fearful for their safety. After the third judge added some questioning, the representative from the Organs of Control office stood and read his summary and recommended a sentence based on the various laws and codes. A couple of times during the proceedings, the courtroom was addressed and asked if anyone had anything to ask or contribute. Since the young men had committed more than two robberies, they were considered professional thieves. From the questioning it was ascertained that one was slightly more culpable than the other, and the Organs of Control representative concluded that the sentence should be three to four years imprisonment for one and four to five years imprisonment for the other.

The judging committee left the court to consider their decision. After a short time, they returned and handed down lighter sentences: three and four years respectively. And by midday it was all over. The boys were allowed to sit with their families for a short time before they were taken away. Despite the language barrier, much of the process had been familiar, although the absence of lawyers gave a directness to the proceedings; the questioning was straightforward, there were no arguments over the finer points of law, of procedure or technical details. The judges gave the boys an old-fashioned dressing-down and reminded them and their families of their social responsibilities.

We asked Minh what future these boys had now, and he told us they would never be allowed back into university, but they may be taught a trade such as carpentry or agricultural work in prison. No doubt life in prison would be hard, but it was believed that rehabilitation was possible and likely, and with family and community support they could be reintegrated into

The interior of my upgraded room at the Post Office Guesthouse.

The view across Tran Quoc Toan Street from my room at the Post Office Guesthouse.

Hung the waiter dressed up for a Tet photo, 1995.

Posing for a Tet photo, 1995. Front: Hung's stepfather and mother. Middle: Hung's Stepsister's daughter. Back: Hung's stepsister and Hung.

Celebrating the Year of the Horse with Minh, my bookshop
partner, 2001.

Rowing with Minh on West Lake, during the Tet, 2001.

Me with Hung
the cyclo driver.

Hung the cyclo driver, his wife, son and niece in their one
room home.

Hung's baby's headstone, Hoang, 1995.

Celebrating the birth of Hung the cyclo driver's daughter, 1996.
His wife and grandmother are in the background.

Mr 'Jazz' Minh.

Saigon wedding. Here I am standing with the bride's mother, bride and groom.

Me with the bride's granny at the wedding party in the countryside.

The day I had
my stolen money
returned at Hoan
Kiem Police
Station. A copy
of this photo was
displayed at the
Police Station.

Diana Van Oort

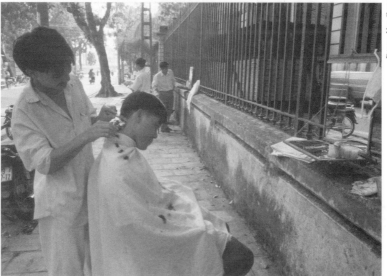

Street Barber, Hanoi.

society—although I suspect the shame would never disappear. In such cases, the families must pay court costs and make restitution to the victims, and they accept this as their moral as well as legal responsibility, although how they can possibly afford to do this is questionable given the low or non-existent salaries of most people. I thought it would be a long time before my friend recovered any of her stolen money, if ever. But as I looked into the tear-filled eyes of the boys' mothers, I knew they would never recover their more significant loss.

As Vietnam takes off economically, the gap between rich and poor is visibly widening every day. Young people, especially, want things they see on television that other young people have. Not long ago, everyone in Vietnam was poor; now things are changing rapidly. The 'open door' policy of 1986 brought an increasing stream of comparatively well-off foreigners to Vietnam. By 1997, it was reported that 19 per cent of people in Hanoi could be considered well-off themselves. Under the circumstances it is easy to understand the temptation to take a short cut. Yet, despite my experience, I still find Vietnam one of the safest countries in the world. I can walk the streets alone, unmolested and unfrightened which, when considering the population density and the stresses in a society undergoing extremely rapid and unprecedented social change, is quite amazing and testament to the strong ethical tradition of the Vietnamese.

For me, the robbery had been quite an experience, filled with twists and surprises. And I was amused to find out years later, that my photo taken with the police the day my money was returned to me still adorned a wall of the Hoan Kiem police station.

A Saigon wedding

The first and most memorable wedding I attended in Vietnam was in Ho Chi Minh City in 1994. I had been sent there from Hanoi for a few months, and in the course of my business there I met Miss Phuong in her capacity as interpreter. After such a brief professional acquaintanceship I was rather taken aback when, only two days after I had met her, she phoned to say she would like to invite me to her wedding. That evening she and her fiancé, Mr Son, personally delivered a written invitation to their wedding to be held a week later and, in typical friendly Vietnamese style, I found myself quickly taken into the bosom of this family. Little did I know then what a marathon event this wedding would turn out to be!

It was arranged that Phuong's younger brother would come to take me to the bride's family home at 10.30am on Saturday morning. I perched on the back of his motorbike, all dressed up in stockings and high heels, handbag and pearls. At their home I was introduced to the family: mother, father, aunts and uncles, cousins, friends and neighbours. Even Phuong herself, not yet dressed in her wedding finery, came downstairs to welcome me. More guests arrived, filling the downstairs living area of their small home, sitting on plastic stools around plastic tables, the men in suits, the women in glittering *ao dai* (a long-sleeved tunic worn over pants) often made of velvet despite the stifling heat.

A constant stream of food began to appear including soup, chicken, salads, small birds' eggs, the specially coloured rice served at weddings, and later brightly coloured sticky desserts and fruit. I was urged to try everything. Each time I emptied my small bowl, someone would drop another delicacy into it. With no-one there who I knew well to help me with the correct protocol, I watched carefully to see how others behaved. As I wondered what to do with the chicken bones I had accumulated in the bottom of my bowl, the matter was swiftly dealt with by the woman sitting next to me. She up-ended my bowl, tipping the contents on the floor behind us, a normal habit apparently, but one that seemed so incongruous to me among these refined and carefully groomed women.

While we were eating, the bride and groom made their first formal appearance, he in a cream double-breasted suit and she in lolly-pink satin, covered with frills and bows, and they promenaded and posed for the video and still cameras under a blinding spotlight for about twenty minutes. After an interval in which eating and drinking continued, the bride and groom returned. This time the bride wore a gold sequined and lamé dress, again with lots of frills, as well as a white veil. More photos were taken and more food and drink served, and the couple now visited all the tables and received envelopes, containing money, from each of the guests. During the austere war time in Vietnam, wedding presents were generally simple and practical: a dish for washing clothes, a thermos for hot water, or other household goods. In these more affluent and materialistic times, money is usually given, not only to start the newlyweds on their life together, but also to pay for the wedding reception. (The same is true of funerals, where, after viewing the body, guests hand an envelope containing money to the family of the deceased to help them pay the costs.) The amount is determined by the closeness of the relationship and the means of the giver, but I always had to seek advice from friends on the correct amount for me to give since foreigners did not fit the normal categories.

By now about four hours had passed and finally the food stopped coming, which meant that the celebrations were over—for that lot of guests at least, but not for the family. Because of the small size of the family home, there were to be two shifts of guests, and after we left the family was going to do it all again! And I also learned that it wasn't over for me either; the groom's family wanted me to attend their celebration and I was told I would be picked up the next morning at 8am.

I was offered a lift home that afternoon by one of the wedding guests (an aunt or a cousin, I think) who seemed very excited by the prospect of meeting a Westerner. Instead of taking me straight home as I expected, she took me via her house, where she dragged out all the family photo albums, which included pages and pages of photos of someone's funeral, complete with photos of the corpse for me to look at. The score so far was one wedding and a funeral! I was exhausted by the time I arrived back at my small room, and as I went through the day's events in my mind that evening, I wondered what the next day would bring.

The next morning the bride's younger brother once again came to collect me at 8am and in a re-run of the previous day we went back to the bride's family home. I was greeted like a close relative by the family as we waited for the arrival of the groom's family, rather well-off Chinese–Vietnamese, who were responsible for the day's celebrations. Marriage ceremonies in Vietnam have three parts. First, the groom's family goes to the bride's family to ask permission for their son to marry the daughter. This usually happens a few weeks before the wedding, but the arrangement can be flexible. In this case, the families must have decided to combine all the ceremonial aspects into one day, so we were gathered here to await the ceremonial arrival of the groom's parents at 9am. We waited and waited until finally, more than an hour late, they pulled up, after having been caught in a traffic jam. Their arrival was heralded by hundreds of ear-splitting explosions from traditional fireworks, followed by a procession of bridesmaids carrying large red and gold painted boxes containing traditional gifts for the bride and her family. These included betel nuts and arnica (the red colour signifying the red of blood and hence the close relationship to be forged), green tea, young rice and lotus seeds. If a dowry has been requested by the bride's parents, that is also included.

Suddenly I found myself dragged into the thick of this crowd and ushered upstairs to the family shrine to witness the second part of the ritual, where incense is burned and ancestors are prayed to. At this part of the ceremony the mother of the bride gives her daughter a gift (in this case a gold chain necklace), whispers a secret to her and tells her she must go to her new family and behave well towards her in-laws. The bride looked very beautiful in her elegant, traditional Vietnamese wedding dress, an *ao dai* of red with gold embroidery.

Once this ceremony was over, all the guests were packed into two minibuses hired for the occasion. The groom's grand-mother seemed rather taken with me and clutched on to me for the next few hours and we were given pride of place in the bus up front near the driver. The first stop was the groom's family home, where we arrived to more loud fireworks, and where we went upstairs for the last part of the wedding ceremony, only to find that the bride had changed into yet another dress—this time a white satin, traditional Western-style wedding dress with pearls and veil. At this ceremony, the bride must pray to the ancestors of her new family and ask their permission to become part of that family. Following light refreshments and a brief sit down on what looked like a brand new vinyl lounge still covered in plastic, it was back on the bus.

For the two days of celebrations I had only the vaguest idea of what was planned. Apart from the bride, who was busy with many duties (not the least of them being constantly changing her outfit), no-one could speak more than a few words of English, and at that stage I could speak almost no Vietnamese. As the second day wore on I wondered where I would end up and if I would ever get home again. It didn't seem to occur to anyone that I might be in the dark about the arrangements, or even have something else to do. Following a couple of futile attempts to ascertain what the plans for the day were, I just gave up and 'went with the flow', a very important technique in surviving in Vietnam, I found.

By now it was early afternoon and after a very long bus ride we ended up out in the countryside at the original village of the groom's family, where it seemed almost the whole village, including its president, was patiently awaiting our arrival for lunch. Another feast was served in the communal hall and again we sat on plastic stools, but this time the men and women were segregated onto separate tables, with the 'aunties' taking me under their wing, while the rowdy 'uncles' took great delight inviting me to their tables to drink toasts and have photographs taken with them. Despite trying to keep a low profile and not overshadow the bride, I was clearly a novelty as the only Westerner in the party.

Suddenly the lunchtime festivities were over and we were herded back on the bus, the men red-faced from too much beer and rice wine. Granny was still clutching my hand. By about 3pm we were back at Phuong's family home, but I still wasn't off the hook! Now I was invited to stay with her family and have a rest for a couple of hours before attending the main party that night. During this waiting time I helped the bride's brother with his English, looked at family photos (no funerals this time), inspected the family table-making business at the back of the house and tried to look relaxed as I lay, as instructed, on a hard wooden bed for a short rest.

At 5pm the minibus arrived loaded with refreshed 'uncles' and off we headed to the centre of Ho Chi Minh City to a large hotel near the river for a formal reception held under a huge multicoloured marquee in the hotel's extensive gardens. As the sun set and the fairy lights appeared, hundreds of guests came streaming in to sit at the large tables, each seating ten to fifteen people. There was food and drink to excess. I couldn't eat any more after two days of feasting and I marvelled at those of our party who could. To begin the evening, the bride wore her white Western-style wedding gown, then changed later into a pale blue satin number. This evening's celebration was clearly not going to be a traditional affair. The repertoire of the professional band and singers hired to perform consisted mainly of Western hits of my youth, such as 'Let's Twist Again' and 'Oh Carol', and the bride herself even took to the microphone for a few songs.

After a few more photos, and a message from one of the uncles (through an interpreter) that he would really like to become my friend, I found myself once again on the back of the bride's brother's motorbike, at last on my way home after a thirteen-hour day. I was exhausted after what had been an extraordinary two-day wedding celebration, one I am not likely to forget or better.

Frogs and snails
and puppy dogs' tails

'Just back from the dog meat restaurant,' I wrote to my mother, not wanting to waste the opportunity to use an opening sentence like that.

'Pam's been to a dog restaurant in Hanoi,' my mother reported to her sister, Eileen.

'How nice,' replied my aunt. 'Fancy them having restaurants where you take your pets!' Hastily, my mother put her straight on who was eating what!

Eating dog meat was not something I really wanted to do. But under the wing of well-meaning Vietnamese friends intent on giving me the full cultural experience of living in Hanoi, I found myself in Nhat Tan dog meat village, being accosted on all sides by restaurant touts extolling the virtues of their particular establishment. I am not sure on what basis my friends selected a particular restaurant, since to me they all looked much the same and most had the same name (*Anh Tu thit cho*), a Vietnamese habit whereby imitators try to trick custom away from long-established businesses. In honour of the fact that a Westerner was included in our group, we were led to a private room—the owner's bedroom, I would guess—where we sat cross-legged on a woven mat on a large wooden bed, with a newspaper tablecloth spread in the centre.

I was told there are up to seven different dog dishes, but thankfully we stopped after five. First there was cold dog; sliced, it looked like cold roast beef. Next came stuffed dog's intestines, a bit like black pudding. Then there were small crumbed balls, which I didn't inquire about, a hot stew with what looked like leg bones poking out to gnaw on, and finally, dog noodle soup. On the side was a stack of dinner-plate-sized rice crispbreads, special green leaves which apparently aided digestion and, thankfully, some beer to wash it down. The taste of dog is quite strong and the meat rather fatty and chewy, but perhaps worst of all were the flies and the barking outside from those destined for next week's menu.

While maybe providing a good traveller's tale, I was certainly not anxious to repeat the dog meat experience. However, at dinner in a Korean restaurant in Hanoi with some Korean associates, I was asked what I preferred to eat.

'Oh, whatever Mr Kim decides will be fine,' I carelessly replied. 'He always orders for me and I can eat anything.'

To which Mr Kim replied, 'You like dog, don't you?'

'Yes,' I answered, thinking I was going along with his joke—until a bubbling stew was served and the penny dropped.

I should have remembered an earlier occasion when an equally careless response had brought on a similar situation. I had been invited to visit Can Tho, in the middle of the Mekong

Delta, a lush and fertile region known as 'the stomach of Vietnam' because of its rich food production. As we travelled along the vast waterway to a small riverside town to have lunch with my colleague's friend, there was an animated discussion among the Vietnamese on board. Finally, my companion turned to me and asked, 'What's the word in English when it isn't an egg but it isn't exactly a bird either?' Understanding slowly dawned as I recalled a conversation not long before where someone talked about being served a special delicacy and how it was soft but had crunchy parts too. Yes, they were planning to serve me duck embryos for lunch! The look on my face must have prompted them to ask, 'Can you eat it?' They looked so disappointed with my answer, so I hastily added, 'but I can eat anything else,' not being able, in my panic, to imagine anything as bad or worse.

My relief quickly turned to horror when lunch was served, however. There on the plate were six turtles, cooked in their shells, little heads and flippers sticking out the holes, looking like grotesque meat pies. Before I could catch my breath, my host had picked one up, and poked and jabbed the meat with a chopstick out through the neck hole, depositing bits of it in my bowl, one piece with its little flipper intact. Actually, the taste was quite okay—a little like chicken, or maybe frog—but I can still see that little flipper in my mind.

After such experiences, I became much more cautious. When someone said they wanted to take me to a 'special' restaurant, I would immediately go on high alert. Once while in Nha Trang, I was told Mr Minh from the post office wanted to take me to a special place for lunch. The menu turned out to be on the walls: not on a blackboard, but literally stuffed exotic species such as civets and other cats and possums, reptiles and birds, nailed or suspended or standing on shelves all around the room.

There are also special duck restaurants, where duck meat floating in blood is served, as well as soup which is actually curdled, solidified duck blood. 'Very good for health,' they tell you, as your own blood drains away at the thought of eating it. And there are goat and deer restaurants, where there always seems to be a small goat or deer tethered out the front. In Australia, a black cat sign outside a shop usually denotes a lottery agency. That is not the case in Hanoi, and at one time, cat restaurants were popping up all over town as the newest craze. It turned out to be short-lived, however, as the government stepped in and banned such restaurants since the depletion of the cat population was having the opposite effect on the rat population. There were also some restrictions imposed on snake restaurants for a while, as the wild snake populations in the rice fields dropped alarmingly, resulting in a rat plague which devastated all the crops.

Unlike dog meat, snake meat is quite tasty and there are even more ways of serving it. As well as snake meat spring rolls, snake rice soup, sautéed snake, snake on the bone and fried balls, there is snake paté, fried snake skin (which is particularly tasty and crunchy), snake broth, snake liver, snake with onions and minced snake balls. The first step on arrival is to select your snake, as the waiter prods and pokes the coiled candidates waiting in a cage. Usually the most active one is selected, and it is quite common for diners to have their photo taken with the snake writhing and wriggling in the catcher's hands. Then the snake is held stretched out and an incision made along the length of its belly, the blood drained into a glass, and the gall and heart deftly removed and placed in separate glasses. Alcohol is added to these glasses and the honoured guest and the host are invited to swallow the heart and gall in one gulp, while the other guests drink the blood and alcohol mix. Later, snake wine is drunk, which is decanted from large glass demijohns containing alcohol and three (and sometimes up to nine) snakes coiled in the bottom. The more snakes, the more valuable the wine, and the rarer the species the better.

Food is an important part of Vietnamese culture and rituals and there are many more words in Vietnamese to describe subtle variations in texture and flavour than in English. There are special foods to celebrate Tet, weddings and funerals and other special occasions, and foods are offered to the gods, too. Once, on a picnic to the Huong Pagoda with a group of devout Vietnamese, we stopped off at every pagoda and small shrine on the way, loading up a tray of food including cooked chicken, small bottles of whisky and packets of cigarettes, offering it to the gods for blessing. After prayers were said the chicken would be packed up again, only to be dragged out once more at the next stop and finally, by this time looking rather bedraggled, eaten by us all for lunch.

One advantage of living in a country where food is a major preoccupation is that it is readily available anywhere and anytime. Vietnamese seem to be constantly 'grazing'. Dawn or midnight, there is always someone with something to sell: a bowl of *pho*, fried banana in batter, sticky rice, fermented pork wrapped in banana leaf, hard-boiled eggs, a cup of tea … Whether you are being rowed through the rice fields and caves at Bich Dong, sailing in Halong Bay or off the coast of Nha Trang, there is usually a small flotilla of craft laden with various wares for sale, everything from fruit, seafood, drinks and chewing gum to embroidered tablecloths. Waiting at a ferry crossing are dozens of sellers eager for your business, pressing bread, biscuits, fruit or cigarettes against the window of your vehicle. Riding on a motorbike through villages at meal times you may be vigorously waved down and urged to eat at the more aggressively entrepreneurial restaurants.

It often helps to have a local guide to assist you in selecting what to try—but not always. My friend Marie was invited out to dinner by a young Vietnamese man hoping to impress her. She explained to him carefully that she didn't eat meat, but when the food appeared, the main dish was clearly not vegetable.

'What do you call this?' she asked him. 'You know I don't eat meat.'

'Oh, it's not meat,' he assured her.

'Then what sort of vegetable is it?'

'It is not a vegetable,' he replied.

'So if it's not animal and not vegetable and clearly not mineral, what is it?' demanded Marie.

'It comes from inside the animal,' he replied innocently, genuinely surprised that his dish of stuffed uterus was not appreciated.

One day Miss Chi from the guesthouse took me to lunch to eat special food, the main ingredient seemingly blood. The street-front part of the eatery was full so we were directed out the back through a small courtyard, past chickens being plucked, vegetables being chopped and noodles being cooked, up some narrow stairs and into a bedroom complete with double bed with a pink satin bedspread and a poster on the wall for Tiger beer. A small wooden table and some stools were put next to the bed for us, and our food was served. Soon after our arrival, a few more customers arrived and more tables and stools were brought in. No-one seemed to think this an odd arrangement, not even when the bed's owner came and hopped into bed, pulled a curtain across and curled up for a lunchtime nap, ignoring a bedroom full of diners.

Sa Pa is a tiny town in Lao Cai province, near the Chinese border and about a twelve-hour road journey north-west of Hanoi. Here is found the highest mountain in Vietnam, some spectacular scenery, fascinating ethnic minority tribes and what turned out to be a generic menu for the town. At the time of my first visit there, tourism was only just beginning and English language speakers were in short supply. In what I imagine was an attempt to overcome this problem, one menu in English was developed and either shared with or plagiarised by every other eating place in town. It took me a little while to fathom this. At first I thought that the first two places I had eaten at must have had some connection and so a common menu. But when I decided to try a small place in the market where locals were eating, I was very surprised to find the same menu, distinctive for its pancakes with banana and chocolate sauce. An inclusion of such an exotic dessert in this poor and isolated community was surprise enough, but to find it on the menu of a dirt-floor shack in the market was beyond belief. This is when I grasped the strategy of the generic menu, because as I pointed to each dish that caught my fancy, the reply was a shake of the head, until I realised that all I was going to get was some rice, and maybe some pork and vegetables—everything else was 'off'.

One of the first restaurants I used to frequent back in 1994 was L'Elegant on Hue Street, just around the corner from where I was living. Often I would be the only customer, so the young waiter, Hung, would use the opportunity to practise speaking English. When another waiter, Kinh, started work there, he brought with him an English song book, containing an odd collection of songs including hits by Abba, the Beatles, Elvis and the Carpenters. They would ask me about the words and the tunes, and before I knew it we were having regular singalongs in the empty restaurant. I will always remember Kinh's last night working there. He had scored a better position in a foreign company, thanks to his improved English, and as I sat eating my steak and fried potatoes he sat opposite me and serenaded me with a moving rendition of 'Love Me Tender'. When I left Ho Chi Minh City after living there for three months in 1994, I took my final meal at the Banana café where I had been a regular customer and one of the staff gave me a farewell, singing 'Unchained Melody', complete with vocal trill, sobs and American intonation.

These days in the major cities of Ho Chi Minh and Hanoi it is possible to find almost any cuisine: there are restaurants serving Japanese, Korean, Malaysian, Singaporean, Mongolian, Italian, Philippine, American fast food, Russian and, of course, French and Chinese cuisine. You can even buy Australian kangaroo and crocodile meat. And many of the newer restaurants themselves are beautiful, situated in renovated French colonial villas or overlooking lakes. But for me there is nothing quite like the experience of eating Vietnamese specialties on the streets, usually sitting on a tiny wooden or plastic stool close to the ground, sometimes with a sheet of plastic overhead in case of rain. No fancy restaurant can rival the flavour of the *banh cuon* with its finely minced pork, mushrooms and herbs wrapped in tissue-thin rice paper and steamed expertly by a lady and her daughters on Ba Trieu Street, or the *pho xau*—sizzling fried beef and noodles—cooked on a hotplate on the pavement of Le Van Huu Street by a man who always wore a little pork-pie hat. Then there is the *pho ga* or chicken noodle soup at Mrs Noodles shop in Nguyen Du Street; the crab noodle soup in Trang Tien lane where motorbikes squeeze past diners and there is often a wait for a free table; and *bun bo* in Hang Dieu Street where flames leap and smoke billows out into the street as more beef pieces are barbequed, ready to add to noodles and vegetables and sprinkled with crushed nuts.

I didn't cook for the eight years I lived in Hanoi. Not only because the food on the streets was so delicious, cheap and readily available, but because you never knew what interesting characters you might meet while sitting there. Some were momentary encounters. Once a bookish-looking man with glasses told me, intriguingly, that he was an army poet.

'The army has poets?' I asked, thinking I had perhaps mis-understood.

'Of course,' he replied before disappearing into the night leaving me to ponder what a working day for him might be like. At lunch one day a young man asked if he could share the table and, after a brief exchange of pleasantries, pronounced with great seriousness, after asking my age, 'You still have your day'. I took this as a rather puzzling compliment. At other times someone might tell you some local history, or maybe share a little of their life story, invite you to their home to meet their family, or arrange to meet again. Hanoi was like one big menu for me: if I wanted duck spring rolls I went to Le Quoc Su Street near the cathedral; if I wanted a French meal I would go to Le Bistrot in Ly Thuong Kiet Street; for ice-cream there was the amazing Bodega café in Trang Tien Street with its grey and dusty fake stalactites and plastic-flower-bedecked grotto; and the best orange juice in town was squeezed by hand by Mrs Tam in her tiny café in Nguyen Du Street, watched on by her darkly handsome husband who apparently gambled away her hard-earned profits.

Who would want to dine alone at home when there were so many adventures, both culinary and social, to be encountered on the streets—the authentic Vietnamese eating experience?

Vilaisan's farewell party

Vilaisan was coming to the end of her three-year term working in Hanoi and wanted to have a big celebration that brought together the many and varied friends she had gathered during that time. There were, of course, many formal do's arranged by her organisation, the Australian embassy, and the various Vietnamese ministries and organisations with which she had worked. But Vilaisan wanted an informal party where her staff could bring their families, where work colleagues could relax without formal social obligations, and where friends she had met outside of work could also come and be farewelled and have one last bash together. During her time in Hanoi, Vilaisan had embraced life with great gusto and enthusiasm, so everyone was expecting her farewell party to be a fun-filled and memorable occasion. Little did we guess just how memorable it would be.

The guest list was diverse. It ranged from government ministers and ambassadors, Australian and Vietnamese bureaucrats and embassy staff, to Vilaisan's ballroom dancing teacher, Mr Dzung, his family and students, her singing group and various individuals whose paths had crossed hers: musicians, students, friends of friends, families of friends, friends of families … Hanoi society is a closely interwoven cloth, where everyone seems related or known to everyone else. Foreigners living in this beautiful city who are prepared to leave the confines of expatriate life and explore what local society has to offer are eagerly taken up by the locals and introduced to the inner life of the city. We were rare birds and valued for being exotic, not condemned for being different as is too often the case in our modern Western societies.

The problem of a venue for the party was suddenly solved when Vilaisan's good friend, Andrea, decided to move out of her small mini-hotel apartment and rent a huge open-plan house with a large paved courtyard. This provided just what Vilaisan was wanting—an informal space, both indoors and outdoors, for a couple of hundred people, where children could play and which wasn't an official facility like the embassy grounds.

Andrea threw herself into the arrangements. She arranged for the local noodle stall lady to come to the party and set up for business in the courtyard, along with the local fresh beer sellers. The local police had also been notified and had given permission for an assembly.

It seemed all the ingredients for a great fun evening had been assembled, but Derek, Andrea's friend and colleague, wanted something more—something for the kids, he said. He could barely contain his excitement when he told Andrea he had arranged for a small troupe from the Hanoi Circus to perform early in the evening—just the thing to entertain the kids and to get the party started, he thought. He would organise everything.

The big day arrived and everything went like clockwork. Andrea arrived home from work just before the guests started to arrive and found five little dogs wearing skirts locked in the bathroom; part of Derek's circus troupe had arrived! The noodle stall lady had set up in the courtyard, complete with little tables and stools and her large cauldron of stock, ready to serve delicious steaming bowls of *pho* throughout the night. The beer sellers were also set up outside under the fairy lights. Inside, Phuong was setting up his electronic keyboard in readiness for the singing group. The first violinist from the Hanoi Symphony Orchestra unexpectedly turned up to give a performance, and Mr Dzung and his ballroom dancing troupe took over the second floor, ready to tango and waltz the night away. The downstairs living area was filled with helium balloons.

Soon the place was bursting with guests and it was time for the entertainment to begin. As the clowns began their act, everyone began gravitating inside from the courtyard, filling every inch of available space. Most of the circus performers in Hanoi were trained by the Russians some years ago, and somehow, despite their Asian faces, they had a Russian look and feel. The clowns were boisterous and quite brutal, and hit each other a lot, to the point that kids were crying, being so close to the action. Next came a bit of juggling, which again was a little worrying given the confines of being indoors and the number of people inside, but there were no mishaps. Then, at last, came the dogs.

Dressed in their little skirts and hats, the dogs went through their routine. Unfortunately, their trainers apparently hadn't considered the effect of a very slippery tiled floor, so these poor little things went slipping and sliding all over the place, hats and skirts askew, trying to gain enough traction to hurl themselves through the hoops. But as the saying goes, 'the show must go on' and could not be modified to suit the conditions. So it was with horror that we watched as the hoops were then doused in petrol and lit, and the dogs rounded up once more to jump, through flames this time.

The circus troupe had not only miscalculated about the floor, but also about the effect of a petrol fire inside an enclosed space somewhat smaller than the usual large circus tent. The audience watched, horrified, as huge clouds of black smoke filled the room and flames leapt towards the two-hundred helium-filled balloons packed up against the ceiling. All that could be heard was the tap-tapping of little dog claws on the tiles as they made their run-up to the flaming rings. In those moments before the dogs jumped, time stretched, motion slowed. I saw in my mind how this scenario could be played out, down to the headlines declaring 'Australians and dogs barbecued in Hanoi!'. And from the frozen expression on Andrea's face as our eyes locked across the crowded room, I knew she was imagining the same. The dogs, however, somehow managed to jump through unscathed. I think it says a lot about living in Vietnam for a long time that we all took it in our stride. None of the little dogs was barbecued, none of the balloons exploded and the ceiling ended up only a little black around the edges.

When all signs of the circus had disappeared and the guests had all gone home, Vilaisan, Andrea and I sat down together and had a cup of tea, reminisced over the good times we had shared, and declared the farewell party a fitting end to an exciting stint in Hanoi. And we all vowed never to leave Derek in charge of entertainment again.

My beautiful,
but brief, singing career

Strangely enough, it actually began when I met a monk in Vientiane, while on holiday with a friend in that tiny capital city of Laos. The 'wats and weavings' tour I named it, since that is about all there is to see—Buddhist monasteries and woven silks. At one of the wats a group of young novice monks in their rust-coloured robes were lounging in the shade of a large spreading tree, looking so picturesque that I couldn't resist taking a photo. Two of the young men broke away from the group to come and talk to my friend and me in their halting English, and insisted on taking us for a tour of their wat. We took more snaps together, exchanged names and addresses, listened to a little of their life stories, and parted with a promise to send copies of the photos.

Novice Bourn Yort, one of the monks, was not planning a lifetime as a Buddhist monk but, like most young men in Laos before they reach marriageable age, was spending some time in a monastery. The duration of this service can range from a few months to a few years, and while the focus is on spiritual matters, it is possible in some monasteries to study more worldly subjects. Bourn Yort was learning English and asked if we could help by sending him some books to study.

It wasn't so easy to find suitable books once we got back to Hanoi, but I managed to put a package together along with copies of the photos I had taken, and sent them off hoping they would make it to the Hysoke *wat*. A painstakingly written thank-you letter arrived weeks later, then a New Year greeting card, and before long it seemed I had acquired a new pen pal. Fossicking around one day in a bookshop in Hanoi looking for something else to send him that might be a bit more interesting than the normal dry old English lesson books I had been sending, I saw a songbook full of popular Western songs. There were old Beatles songs, Elvis classics, songs by The Eagles, The Carpenters, Lionel Ritchie, even Abba, who were still on their first wave of popularity in Indochina. Knowing how much young people in Asia enjoy and want to know about Western pop culture, I guessed this would be quite a hit at the monastery. And it tickled me to imagine these serious young men with religious robes and shaven heads crooning away, wondering about yellow submarines and blue suede shoes.

So how does this connect to the start of my singing career? Before I wrapped up the book to send, I started leafing through it and before I knew it, there in my little room in Hanoi, I was in full swing, belting out song after song from the last four decades, amazed by what was retained in the recesses of my brain. After a couple of hours I was hoarse and dry, but on such a high! It reminded me of how good singing used to feel and how I hadn't sung for years. I had sung at home to my kids when they were small, but when they reached about eleven or twelve years old it was clearly an embarrassment to them for me to be singing songs from the musicals while washing up together, so I stopped singing altogether.

One of the things I had been struck by in Vietnam was the natural way people sang in the course of daily life: street sellers walking along singing quietly to themselves, women cleaning their houses. Parties always involved some singing, and even business deals did too, sometimes. If handed a microphone or invited to a karaoke room, everyone—from the most serious-looking high-level official to the shyest, most demure young girl—turned into a performer, bellowing forth heroic revolutionary battle songs or sugary sweet love songs. Once, I went on an official visit to the Hai Phong Post Office company with a group from the Hanoi Post Office and we were greeted by song. Our group readily responded, and for twenty minutes, songs were traded back and forth. Whenever I was asked for a contribution in these situations, I would die. Even if I could get a sound, however terrible, to come out from my constricted throat, *what* could I sing? 'Waltzing Matilda'? 'Click go the shears'? Where was our equivalent of the hundreds of songs about Hanoi? Hanoi in the spring, the summer, the winter, autumn; the red heart of Hanoi; songs about the pavements of Hanoi, the smells of Hanoi, the flowers of Hanoi. 'I still call Australia home'? How long could I go on declining the invitation to share in this social pleasure?

At this point I had the first two elements to get me started: I had remembered and felt once again the physical pleasure of singing (apparently caused by the release of those wonderful endorphins) and I was living in a society where singing was expected and appreciated. That is, I had motivation, reason and opportunity. All that remained was the fortuitous meeting with the wonderful Mr Quy Duong.

I was at the opening of my friend Minh's new jazz club and began chatting with a Swedish woman sitting next to me. She had just come from a singing lesson, she said, with a Vietnamese teacher who was wonderful. It took me a few weeks to get up the courage, but I decided to contact her teacher and see if I could join a singing group or get a small group of friends together for lessons.

Quy Duong was quite definite when I spoke to him on the phone. Individual lessons were essential, not group lessons, and we could start that week. He would come to my house and the cost was US$7 per hour. Then I discovered that Quy Duong was in fact the director of the Hanoi Opera and Dance Company and an honoured People's Artist, who had studied abroad for many years and was famous for singing patriotic songs during the war against the United States. What had I done?

He arrived exactly on time on his Honda Dream II motor-bike. While walking through the door, and before speaking, he began his warm-up vocal exercises; 'Meeee, me, me, me, me,' echoed around my walls. 'Now you,' he commanded. I began a stammering explanation about how I couldn't sing to save my life and this was probably a bad idea and I was sorry to waste the time of someone of his stature. Calmly, he spoke to me in rather Russian-accented English. 'Anyone can sing. Now, take courage. Big breath!' And that was that. I began. And I continued to find the courage because of his great kindness, patience and amazing tolerance. It must have been awful for him, a teacher who had taught and worked with the country's most talented singers, having to listen to my dreadful screeches. But he was always so encouraging and so happy to be teaching me Vietnamese songs.

At the outset I tried some classics like 'I'm in the Mood for Love', 'Sunny Side of the Street' and 'Summertime', the only English music he had at that time. Later I had friends send me some Andrew Lloyd Webber scores. The problem was that under Quy Duong's direction they all ended up sounding like heroic marches. There was no room for interpretation and variation as he conducted me in strict regular time. Where I imagined a sexy smouldering rendition, I ended up with a staccato: 'Hup two three four … I'm / in the mood for / love, two three four …'

I eventually realised I wasn't going to convert Quy Duong to a more relaxed, informal way of singing, so I decided it would be more fun to learn some Vietnamese songs to pull out when necessary at social occasions. And it proved to be an extremely popular party trick. The quality of my voice didn't seem to matter to the audience; it was the feeling in the heart and the fact that a foreigner was singing in their language that mattered to them.

I looked forward to my lessons. My teacher would encourage me to breathe deeply and sing with a 'big voice'. And it felt good! Oddly enough, I was never quite as brave without him there, and his pleasure was always so great I could almost believe for a few moments that I sounded good. I knew I didn't (and this isn't false modesty—I have a tape to prove it!) but because my teacher was always so positive, I felt good. Years later, when talking about some of his students, he said diplomatically, 'Madame Melinda has a beautiful voice, and Madame Pam [me] has a very good ear.'

Over the months I built up a small repertoire of Vietnamese classics. It wasn't easy to learn the words and I would often walk about the streets muttering under my breath trying to learn by rote. It wasn't easy to learn the tunes, either. I usually had no musical score for these songs, just Quy Duong's hand-written words, and there was no musical accompaniment. He would sing and I would have to remember the tune line by line. As the songs became longer and more complex, I had to use a tape recorder to remind me of the tunes. As I listen to those tapes now (and I can only bear short bursts), I am again amazed at and grateful for Quy Duong's patience.

Lessons had an unpredictability about them. Not only was I unsure what song we would be studying, but I was never sure who else might come along with him. One day my teacher arrived with a young man on the back of his motorbike carrying a huge electronic keyboard. This was his son, Phuong, who would play for me so I could get the feel of how to 'perform' a song I had finally mastered. A talented classical pianist and budding jazz musician, Phuong is now furthering his career in the United States, but at that time he was happy to come along occasionally to my lessons and provide some musical backing.

On another occasion, Quy Duong brought an old woman along to listen to me. Ignoring my acute embarrassment, he went on to describe the woman's illustrious singing career and then ordered me to sing my repertoire for her. In fact, it turned out to be a delightful hour as we sang along together, all three of us, and they reminisced, and no-one really cared that my voice wasn't up to scratch. A variation on this would be for my teacher to take me to his next lesson. I might find myself in some small community hall with a group of kids, being introduced as if some sort of celebrity and being expected to sing for them.

After only two lessons, I found myself featuring in a documentary about Quy Duong being made for Vietnamese television to celebrate his sixtieth birthday. Just before my lesson was due to start, a young woman came to my door, but as her English was poor and she was clearly nervous speaking to me, I had no idea what she was saying. I noticed that she was carrying a microphone in its box and thought maybe she wanted to sell it. As I was trying to figure out what she wanted, two young men drove up carrying a large video camera and other equipment. Fortunately Quy Duong arrived at that moment and ushered them into my house. 'Yes, yes,' he said, 'they want to make a film about my life, and part of my life these days is teaching foreigners in Hanoi to sing. We will just have our normal lesson and later she might ask you some questions.'

And with that he started me on my warm-up exercises as the three strangers began setting up their equipment to film us. I wasn't sure what I should be more embarrassed about: the fact that my singing, after only a couple of lessons, would be broadcast on national television; that I wasn't looking my best, with no make-up and old house clothes on; or the fact that I had just noticed the background to all their shots would show my underwear strung out on the line to dry!

I never saw the film. I had asked when it would be shown but no-one could ever tell me, But I know that it was shown on national television and I wasn't left on the cutting room floor, because some months later when I was teaching a class of MBA students at the Business School of the National Economics University, my students told me they had seen me in it. They didn't mention if they had seen my washing in the background!

When you live alone in a foreign country for some time it is possible to reinvent yourself. You have none of your normal social conventions to hold you back, and you don't have to worry about embarrassing your parents or children, partner or friends. If your adopted country is Vietnam, you have even more scope to play with. Vietnamese are so curious and interested in foreigners, and are extremely tolerant. One of my friends had noticed that every day for the year she had been living in her house, an old Vietnamese man sat across the road watching her. One day she asked him why he was always watching her. He replied that he found everything she did interesting. And that's how it is—foreigners, especially Westerners, are just interesting. Not only interesting, but we are told we are young and beautiful, or tall and handsome according to gender, and talented, even in the face of contrary evidence. Heady stuff! Especially when you come from a country like Australia, where even slightly-above-average height poppies are quickly cut back, where stepping into the smallest circle of limelight exposes you to criticism of being 'up yourself' and where the required reply to the question 'What do you know?' is 'Not much'. We know that our children need a supportive and kind environment to develop and stretch, but we don't extend this to adults. In Vietnam, I had an 'embarrassment by-pass' and it felt great! And it was just as well, because I was soon to make my public singing debut.

Dien Bien Phu is a long way from Broadway. It is even a long way from Hanoi. This remote town is almost as far west as you can go from Hanoi before being in Laos. Yet it played a crucial role in the modern history of Vietnam, for it was here on 7 May 1954 that the Vietnamese nationalist soldiers defeated the French army and thus ended French colonial rule in Vietnam. The French believed their garrison impregnable, surrounded as it was by steep mountains. However, under the command of General Vo Nguyen Giap, the Vietnamese dismantled their heavy artillery, hauled it in pieces over the mountain any way they could, reassembled it on the other side and surrounded the French, making it impossible for them to receive supplies or reinforcements. To celebrate the anniversary of this great Vietnamese victory, Quy Duong was taking a group of thirty-six singers, dancers, musicians and technicians from the Hanoi Opera and Dance Company on the road to perform two concerts at Dien Bien Phu. And he invited me to come along.

By car or bus it takes about two days to get there, provided there are no mishaps along the way—but the poor condition and steepness of the roads means there are almost always mishaps. After the two concerts in Dien Bien Phu, the group planned to stop at some other towns on the way back to Hanoi and give concerts there. This seemed like it would be a bit too much for me to cope with; I knew what travel was like in this region and guessed (correctly, as it turned out) that the buses they would be using would be very old school-type buses with hard seats and no airconditioning. I also knew that food and accommodation in these remote regions would be a challenge. So I decided I would fly to Dien Bien Phu and meet the group there on the Tuesday, then fly back to Hanoi on the Friday, allowing me to be at both concerts on the Wednesday and Thursday nights.

The flight only takes fifty minutes with Vietnam Airlines, but we had some trouble getting off the ground. We were late boarding, then the engine wouldn't start so we were bussed back to the terminal to wait some more. Finally, we touched down at Dien Bien Phu more than one hour late, only to be informed before leaving the terminal that Friday's return flight had been cancelled. I expect the airline didn't tell us before we left Hanoi in case we decided not to go!

Quy Duong was waiting for me at the airport and took me back to the guesthouse where the company was staying. After giving me something to eat, he sent me off to my room to have a rest; over the next few days I did a lot of resting in my room. For history buffs it might be interesting to retrace the steps of this famous military campaign and to stand near the famous landmarks—the bunker where the French General de Castries surrendered, hill A1 which is apparently much smaller than everyone imagines—and visit the various monuments and museum. But once done, there is not much else to do and the thought of being trapped in Dien Bien Phu at the mercy of Vietnam Airlines' unreliable schedule did not make me feel easy. The open spaces of a huge flat plain surrounded by mountains and the blue skies and white fluffy clouds were a welcome change from the high-density living and depressing grey of Hanoi. But you can walk the entire town in about thirty minutes and not find anything you want to do there. I was starting to wonder if de Castries surrendered just to get out of the place.

It was much more fun back at the guesthouse, where there were five tenors, a dancing troupe, musicians and even a transvestite comedian. And the roadies were like roadies everywhere, testing microphones and worrying about their equipment, which included electronic keyboards, guitars, drums, saxophone, huge speakers and full lighting system, and even laser lights and smoke machines. It reminded me of those old movies—not exactly a Judy Garland and Mickey Rooney one, more like Margaret Rutherford and Alec Guinness playing repertory actors staying at seedy guesthouses where you come upon someone rehearsing at every turn. There would be ballerinas in one area, folk dancers in another, and in lounge rooms and along corridors, singers would be learning the words of yet another song about a famous victory. One of the books I had brought along with me was Peter Carey's *The Unusual Life of Tristan Smith,* but reading it in this environment, his life seemed not so 'unusual'. I was reading about a circus while being in one, it seemed!

The first concert, held on Wednesday night, was an open-air public concert and a bit of a warm-up for the following night. But the group didn't hold back on the special effects and the locals were awestruck by the laser light display, and at times the smoke belching from the smoke machines completely obscured the performers. The next night's performance was held in the town hall and the place was packed with all the province officials, VIPs and their families and anyone who could get a ticket or climb through a window.

That day, Quy Duong had informed me that I was to sing in the main concert the next night. I probably should have guessed this would happen; there's no such thing as a free invitation to Dien Bien Phu! It was decided that because there was only a short time for me to learn and remember the words, I would join the five tenors in the chorus of a famous song about how the Vietnamese hauled the cannons over the mountains to defeat the French. I had to shout alone at various points *'Hai, ba nao'*, the equivalent of 'Heave ho', then the others would join in and hopefully conceal any of my mistakes. I was given a copy of the words, about fifteen minutes of practice, and only heard the musical accompaniment when I was on stage doing it.

Everyone was so excited as we headed off for the town hall, me in the car with Quy Duong, the others in the two yellow buses. Once we got there, I was told to sit in the front row of the audience and wait. There was no program and no-one seemed to know when or if I was going on stage. As the only non-Vietnamese person there, I was already creating interest among the audience. The concert had been going for more than one hour when finally Quy Duong came over to me to say I would be on in a few minutes. After he had sung two songs he would introduce me, and I was then to walk up the front steps of the stage. And not only was I to sing the song we prepared with the tenors, but also do a solo of a song I had already learnt that was almost a national song, called 'Vietnam, Ho Chi Minh'.

I have some photos to prove that I did it, and there are some frozen moments indelibly etched in my memory—the looks on the faces of the other singers when it seemed I wasn't going to get the first words out, the glare of the spotlights blinding me to the audience, and the feeling of terror when I couldn't quite recognise the tune as played by the musicians and couldn't hear myself. I must have been okay because the crowd went wild, not because I sang well, but because I was a Westerner dressed in an *ao dai*, the Vietnamese national dress, singing much-loved Vietnamese songs in the middle of nowhere. As I said, it may have been a long way 'off Broadway', but it was quite a singing debut. The next day when I went walking in the town, I was a celebrity. Quy Duong had given me quite an introduction, telling them where I was from, my age, how many children I had, the work I had done. Now I was hearing it all repeated back to me as locals talked together about 'the old foreign woman who sang last night dressed in an *ao dai*' and invited me to drink tea with them.

I have never sung publicly again and have no plans to ever do so. After all, it's hard to top having played at the Dien Bien Phu Town Hall as part of one of the most famous celebrations in the country. My next challenge was to get out of Dien Bien Phu as soon as possible.

I checked with Vietnam Airlines to confirm that the Friday flight was definitely cancelled. When I asked about Saturday's flight the girl said wistfully that she 'hoped' it would come, but even if it came, it might not take off again if the weather conditions—notoriously fickle and dangerous here because of the geography of the high mountains surrounding the town—were not favourable. The idea of spending many more days there was not appealing, so I began to arrange a back-up plan.

In my previous job with the VNPT, I had come to know the company's directors, deputy directors and other officials from just about every provincial post office in the country. It seemed that wherever I went in Vietnam, I met someone I knew or who recognised me. On the day I arrived in Dien Bien Phu I ran into the driver from Lai Chau Province Post Office who insisted that I visit the director and bring Quy Duong with me. None of the Vietnamese in our group from Hanoi knew anyone in town and here was I introducing them to the locals.

At the Dien Bien Phu Post Office, I was assured there would be a seat for me in the mail van driving to Hanoi if the plane didn't arrive on Saturday. It wasn't an option I was looking forward to, as I had experienced a much shorter trip in a mail van from Lang Son province, north of Hanoi near the Chinese border, back to Hanoi. Then, the normal two- to three-hour trip stretched to about eight hours as we stopped at every little post office on the way and picked up and dropped off various friends and relatives needing transport. The only consolation was it would be faster than going back with the performers, who had a concert tour planned.

Fortunately I didn't need to take up either offer. The plane arrived and weather conditions were perfect for flying. I got a lift to the airport in the local ambulance with a French female doctor who had been staying at the same guesthouse while working at the local hospital for a French aid organisation. But I was on such a high I almost didn't need a plane to fly home! I had had my fifteen minutes of fame.

My lessons continued and my repertoire expanded to the point where I didn't think I could remember any more. The idea that one day I would have forgotten all these songs I had struggled so hard to learn prompted me to investigate recording myself. I did some experiments at home with a small recorder and was amazed at the level of noise pollution in Hanoi. The cacophony of sounds from traffic, horns, construction sites and street sellers all but drowned out my singing. So with the help of Quy Duong's son, I rented the recording studio at the School of Music.

I wasn't quite what I had in mind. There was an old piano and some old recording equipment, the microphone looking like something the Andrews sisters might have used. No magic technology to enhance and conceal, or soften the roughness of my poor attempt. And we had to get all ten songs finished in about an hour, so not too many second takes were allowed. Quy Duong was there to conduct and encourage me, his son to play the piano. There is only one copy of the tape in existence; I gave it to my parents for a Christmas present that year, but only after exacting the promise that they were never to play it for anyone else.

Life got a bit busy after my recording session and I never got back to having any more lessons. Quy Duong was getting ready to retire, his son was getting ready to go to America to study music, and I couldn't imagine how I could top my singing experiences. After the success of my recording session, Quy

Duong regularly took his students to record themselves for fun. And whenever I went to visit him, we always reminisced about our performance at Dien Bien Phu, with him insisting that I sing again for him with a 'big voice' and courage.

Last tango in Hanoi

If on a visit to Vietnam you are expecting to see endless vistas of rice fields, workers in conical hats and beautiful young girls with long black hair and straight backs wearing traditional Vietnamese *ao dai*, then you certainly won't be disappointed. All those clichéd images, and more, that you find in travel guides and films hit you in the face the moment you arrive in Vietnam—the French colonial architecture, motorbike-jammed streets, fruit sellers shouldering their heavy baskets of produce, sidewalk noodle shops, the pictures and busts of Ho Chi Minh, incense-filled pagodas. Of the other dominant images the West has of Vietnam—those depicting the horror and tragedy of war—there is surprisingly little evidence outside of museums, if you don't include the vast number of cemeteries. Certainly, the smiles and friendliness you receive give no hint of past conflict and suffering.

But what may really surprise and seem incongruous to many expecting only to see these stereotypical scenes, is the large and growing interest in classical ballroom dancing, especially Latin-American dancing, among young and old alike. In Hanoi and

Ho Chi Minh City, it is possible to go ballroom dancing every night of the week (and even mornings and afternoons) and the provincial cities also have their share of dance halls and dancing devotees, waltzing and cha-cha-ing enthusiastically.

My first glimpse of this dancing world came when some staff from the Hanoi Post Office with whom I had been working in 1994 took me along to one of their regular twice-weekly dancing lessons, arranged and paid for by the Post Office. Mr Son, who was too shy to actually participate himself, drove me on his motorbike to a small, dusty, tiled room cleared of most furniture except for a few chairs around the edge, where I joined about twenty students who were following their teacher in some basic rumba and cha-cha steps, muttering '*mot, hai, mot, hai*' (one, two, one, two) as they shuffled around the room. Once the rudiments had been mastered, the music was turned on, partners were taken and as feet untangled and bodies relaxed into the rhythm, I began to really enjoy the experience. Admittedly, dancing the rumba in a run-down room with a small Vietnamese man wearing plastic sandals was hardly reminiscent of Dorothy Lamour in a sarong in the arms of a handsome hero under gently swaying tropical palms and a Hollywood moon, but it did serve to remind me of the pleasure that dancing can bring. So some time later, when my matchmaking friend Mrs Thanh suggested I go dancing with her friend Mr Kim, I was ready to try.

Mrs Thanh wouldn't go dancing herself, fearing that it would somehow compromise her reputation, but it was quite acceptable for her friend Mr Kim to go dancing every night. I later discovered that Mr Kim had taken the trouble to learn some English especially for the occasion so that he could ask me, 'Would you like to dance?', 'Would you like something to drink?' and say 'Wait me, please', when he went to park and later collect his motorbike. This limited vocabulary turned out to be quite adequate, since the whole time was spent dancing and I was busy concentrating on what my feet were doing as Mr Kim whirled me through the rumba, cha-cha, waltz, mambo, tango and bebop.

The dancing hall we went to was in Tang Bat Ho Street and was a large, ugly circular concrete building with a tiled floor. Chairs and tables were arranged around the perimeter of the room and a small band consisting of keyboard, drums, guitars, trumpet and singer played on the stage. Dancers ranged from the elderly to teenagers; I was introduced to a famous dancing teacher—the 'old professor of dancing' I was told—who, at eighty-five years, was still dancing every night and who looked fitter than men half his age as he waltzed and discoed with equal agility. The 'young professor of dancing' was also there most nights. He sported permed hair and wore his shirt open to show off a gold medallion on a hairless chest, as he whirled and twirled his frilled and sequined partner about the dance floor. Some of the older women wore traditional Vietnamese dress while the young girls tried to emulate the fashions of their latest pop idol, but everyone participated in all the dances whether a slow waltz or a disco.

The routine was unvarying: the first dance was the *paso doble* at 8.30pm on the dot. At 9.20pm the band would take a break and taped disco music would be played for twenty minutes. The last dance was always a Viennese waltz at 10.30pm, and as the final bars of the 'Blue Danube' hung in the air, the dancers had their coats on and were out the door and on their motorbikes. Nobody ever stayed on the dance floor waiting for the next dance to begin. At the end of each dance, Mr Kim would give me a final twirl, we would then push our way back to our chairs and just as I was about to sit, the music would strike up again and, as if this was totally unexpected, Mr Kim would ask if I would like to dance this dance. Off we would go again, jostling our way back to the dance floor.

No doubt an important reason for this enthusiasm was that until quite recently, dancing had been banned by the Vietnamese government. In the years before 1954, dancing was common among middle- and upper-class Vietnamese, especially in Hanoi. After that time, when the communists took power, dancing stopped, and until the early 1980s there was no public dancing, no public playing of European or Latin-American music allowed. Anyway, most people had no time or money, or probably energy, to go dancing. Survival was the focus of everyone's attention in those dark days.

I met Ty and her husband Hau at the Tang Bat Ho Street dancing club where they were to be found dancing twice a week. Even though they were in their seventies, they were still entering dance competitions. Marriage, six children and government bans hadn't stopped their dancing. Back in the 1940s, Ty's sister married a Chinese man, who taught Ty to dance and would sometimes take her to the dancing clubs then operating in Hanoi. These clubs were only available to the upper and well-off middle classes, as it could cost as much as half a week's salary to enjoy a night of dancing, often to the music of Filipino musicians. When these clubs closed their doors in later years under an austere communist rule, there were only private opportunities for dancing, when friends and family might gather for a special occasion such as Tet or a birthday. They would turn on the record player softly, draw the curtains and dance at home behind closed doors.

Change began in 1978 when a large delegation of young Vietnamese people was sent to Cuba for a festival and gathering of youth from all over the socialist world. On the final day of that event, a closing celebration was arranged with lots of eating, drinking, singing and dancing—dancing in which the Vietnamese contingent couldn't participate. Unhappy at this state of affairs, the leaders of the delegation approached the government on their return to Vietnam and asked them to pay attention to this matter. As the new decade opened, the government lightened its approach and lifted the ban on dancing, but there was a problem; the skill and knowledge of dancing had almost disappeared. So old people who could recall the steps from the French colonial times, and Vietnamese from the South who had had contact with the West, were called into service to teach dancing, and long-forgotten tunes were heard once more.

The 'open door' policy of 1986 provided further impetus to this interest, but even at that time still only a few could enjoy the pleasures of the dance—only those who could afford lessons, who could afford even the low entry fee to the dancing clubs, and who could afford proper shoes and suitable clothes. But by the 1990s a sizable number of Vietnamese could do just that and the dance business boomed.

Mr Dzung, who was to become my teacher, gave up his career as a doctor in a large hospital in Hanoi to become a full-time dancing teacher and found happiness, good medicine for everyone, he believes. 'When I dance I forget everything,' he says with feeling, having more to forget than most of us after enduring many years of extreme hardship as a soldier in the army during the worst years of the Vietnam war. Passionate about dancing after having been introduced to it by his father when just a small child, Dzung is unusual for his generation, who never had an opportunity to dance when they were young, being caught in the terrible years of war, followed by years of isolation and hard-line communist doctrine.

Dzung's father, Nga, was born in 1918 and began dancing around 1940 when he was still single and working under the French in the railway department. Stationed in the busy northern port city of Hai Phong, he learnt some dance steps from his friends and would then go to the dancing clubs to practise with the professional dancing girls there. Many of these girls had come from Hong Kong, Shanghai and other parts of China hoping to escape from the Japanese invaders, and they brought with them the knowledge of dance. At these clubs, men would buy dance tickets and the girls would later be paid by the owner of the club according to the number of tickets they had collected.

In 1942, Nga moved back to Hanoi, and after marrying there, his dancing was curtailed. But even when dancing became forbidden in public after 1954, Dzung's father kept the skill alive, despite great hardship and reduced family circumstances, by transferring his love of dancing and music to his young son, teaching him steps and rhythms in the privacy of their home. Dzung's older sister can remember her father dancing around their home with Dzung as a baby in his arms. Dzung himself remembers being taught some simple steps as a ten-year-old and listening to the different dance rhythms. 'Lucky to have a father like that,' he says with emotion—a father who encouraged him to go out dancing and who managed to keep some of his dancing shoes through the lean years and eventually hand them on to his son at a time when few, even in Hanoi, had proper shoes. Dzung continued the family tradition by teaching his young son some dance steps, although these days it can be done very publicly. He is also in great demand at schools to teach young students to dance. And in the ultimate twist of irony, he was asked to teach dancing to the staff of the Ministry of the Interior, an organisation whose task it once was to police the ban on dancing.

Dzung's father can no longer dance as his legs are too weak, but occasionally he likes to go along to watch the dancers and listen to the music. The last time he went, though, he complained that the lighting effects were not what they once were, when they would change colour according to the dance—red for the tango, blue for a waltz—to set the mood. When asked why he loved dancing so much, he answered that it was good for health: good exercise and a chance to enjoy music at the same time. His son also believes in the benefits of dancing, claiming that he 'is still practising medicine, only in a different way'. Dancing allows you to keep fit, he says, but ballroom dancing, unlike modern disco dancing, requires a partner and this, he argues, provides an additional benefit because 'you can make friends, dance with someone you like and relax more with a partner than alone and enjoy music together'.

I first met Dzung at the Tang Bat Ho Street dancing club. As the only foreigner there I was viewed as something of a novelty and was flattered and fussed over, but not by Dzung, who wasted little time in telling me that others might think I danced well, but in fact I needed some lessons to improve my technique, and he was just the teacher to do it! And so it came to pass; twice a week after work, Dzung would come to my small flat with his cassette player, we would move the furniture out of the way and I would dance for ninety minutes with a man I hardly knew. Soon I became obsessed with dancing: I would wake up each morning with the sounds of tango and rumba music inside my head, and would look forward to the group practise sessions held by Dzung on Saturday afternoons in a small school hall he rented.

I took Dzung along to a friend's house-warming party one evening after one of my lessons and, following our impromptu dancing demonstration, he had everyone signing up for lessons. I had started a trend and Dzung was in high demand. The Australian embassy arranged classes for their staff, both local and expatriate. Dancing lessons were included in Australian training programs for students planning to study overseas. My colleagues at work arranged private lessons to be held on the rooftop of their apartment building, and they still reminisce about dancing the tango under a Hanoi moon to the strains of 'The Isle of Capri' played to a tango beat.

My favourite memory is of the first time three male work colleagues came to Dzung's Saturday afternoon practise session. The Vietnamese who attended were an interesting group of young and old, some were journalists, others were doctors who had worked in unusual locations like Algeria and the Congo, and they spoke a number of languages. One old doctor took the three newcomers under his wing when he saw they were having trouble with their steps. He placed them in a line holding hands to practise, with himself in the middle. Then, when it seemed they had got it, the doctor would sweep one up in his arms and, dancing the role of the woman, lead the newcomer around the floor, then come back for another. Poor Jess, a twenty-four year old American graduate student, was red-faced with embarrassment, but after it was over admitted sheepishly that he had really enjoyed the afternoon.

Dancing fever was still in full swing when Olivia came to Hanoi with her video camera. She was looking for a subject for the ABC-TV program 'Race around the World', a competition in which six contestants were sent to ten places of their choice anywhere in the world to make a series of five-minute documentaries. Vietnam was Olivia's ninth country in the competition, with only Japan to go, and she was doing well. On the night she arrived in Hanoi I happened to meet her and suggested that Dzung and ballroom dancing would make a good subject. So off we went to talk to Dzung and his father, and a few days later we went to the Tang Bat Ho dancing club. Olivia's film was a big hit with the judges and she eventually went on to win the overall competition. The night it was aired on Australian television, Dzung and his family were invited to watch it at the Australian embassy and a small dancing party was held there afterwards to celebrate.

Dzung's extended family—his mother and father, his wife and son, his brother and his family—were all squeezed into a few rooms of a run-down French colonial house, all they were allowed to keep of their home after the communists came to power. Dzung had built a tiny room in the roof to use as a dance studio. Access was by ladder from the kitchen and only those less than about 175 centimetres tall could stand upright in it. The floor was covered with linoleum and a large mirror was affixed to one of the end walls. There he kept his collection of dance music tapes, some videos of dancing competitions and a prized copy of an old dancing book written in Bulgarian that his brother helped him translate and which he would pore over for hours, studying the steps in detail and practising in front of his mirror.

I had promised Dzung to look for more up-to-date dancing books during a trip to Beijing, but all I managed was to get caught up in a dancing group in the park outside the Temple of Heaven early one morning where an old woman grabbed me for a tango, an old man taught me the Beijing two-step, and a passing Korean tourist expertly waltzed me around. My friends in Australia didn't know anything about dancing and at that time the Internet was not available in Vietnam, so I didn't know where to go to get him the information he needed to improve his knowledge of modern ballroom dancing. But then a chance encounter in Kuala Lumpur changed Dzung's life.

On the way back to Vietnam, after spending a couple of weeks with my family in Australia, I decided to stop over in Kuala Lumpur for a few days to see my friend Mrs Thanh, who was now teaching Vietnamese at the university there. I was delighted to find she had been taking dancing lessons and one night she and some friends arranged to take me dancing. Mr Ong drove us about thirty kilometres from the city to a place which seemed in the middle of nowhere. On one side of the road next to some fields was a small Muslim prayer hall, full of worshippers. On the other side was an open-air dancing club with brightly lit Carlsberg beer signs and flashing lights, and a dance floor surrounded by tables and chairs, with a roof but no walls. It was almost deserted when we arrived at 9.30pm but began to fill up at 10pm, a time when Hanoian dancers are thinking about heading home. Our driver, Mr Ong, didn't dance himself, but he found some more friends for us to dance with. I learnt that a group of them had just come from being tested, for their bronze medal in dancing jive, by an Imperial Society of Teachers of Dancing (ISTD) examiner from London. Serendipitously, one of them had the examiner's business card with him. Here at last was a contact. And what a contact she turned out to be.

Posing with Minh, my bookshop partner, on his motorbike at
Hoan Kiem Lake.

Me with Mr Dzung posing for a formal photo.

Me and
Mr Dzung
dancing at
Tang Bat Ho
dancing club.

Mr Nga (Mr Dzung's father) standing near a photo of
himself as a young man.

Mr Dzung teaching his son to dance in the park.

Inside
The Bookworm.

Outside
The Bookworm
in Ngo Van So
Street.

The Cuong

Street dining.

Drinking a special rice wine made in Hoa Binh province
through bamboo straws.

Drinking snake blood mixed with alcohol at the snake
meat restaurant.

Mrs Noodles and her 22 cooked chickens on Nguyen Du Street.

The Cuong

Posing at the
Uncle Ho statue
factory.

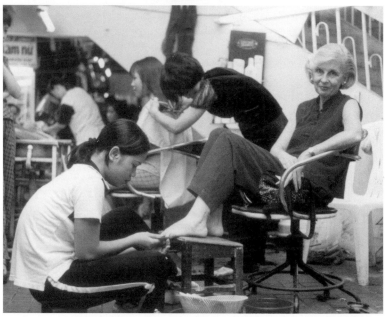

The Cuong

Having a pedicure at the Hom market in Hanoi.

As an examiner for ISTD, Marion Brown had travelled to many countries such as China, Malaysia, Poland, Thailand and Taiwan, running workshops for teachers and conducting examinations. She was so taken with the plight of Dzung, struggling away with his outdated Bulgarian dancing book, that she offered to make a side trip from Bangkok to Hanoi to see Dzung at her own expense when on her next Thai assignment, if I could just find her some accommodation. A friend at the Australian embassy, another keen ballroom dancer, had a large comfortable apartment and was happy to put Marion up there.

Dzung was beside himself with excitement, and so was I. Marion sent me the official ISTD ballroom and Latin-American dance technique books, which are the bible to dancing teachers. They describe in precise detail the positions of the feet, the exact amount of turn, the rise and fall, correct holds and timing. I became Dzung's collaborator, helping him interpret and understand the terms used, and we would spend hours discussing the technical points of heel turns, heel pulls and heel pivots as we prepared for Marion's visit.

At last Marion arrived in Hanoi. After a couple of days of lessons to clarify and explain the finer points and to assess Dzung, she decided he was ready to take the ISTD Latin-American teacher exam at the Associate level. After so many years of labouring away alone, Dzung proudly became Vietnam's first ISTD Associate member.

The days when the club in Tang Bat Ho Street was the premier dancing venue and crowded on Friday, Saturday and Sunday nights, and reasonably full on other nights, passed. Patrons began to want more sophisticated surroundings, with the trendsetters in town deciding on the newest 'in' place and the crowds follow. For a while it was the Magnetic Club where even on weekdays, the 3.30pm to 6.30pm afternoon dancing sessions were crowded with students, retirees and workers who managed to escape their shops or offices for an hour or two. When it closed temporarily for renovations to expand the dance floor, the crowd moved to Metal, which had started out as a disco club but found a bigger market in ballroom dancing. For a while the wonderfully named Up and Down Club, said to be financed by the Russian mafia and located on the fifth floor of a ten-pin bowling alley, was popular. Some nights there would be a Russian floorshow to help attract the crowds, and the 10am Sunday morning dancing session was also popular. Dozens of other clubs came and went, or waxed and waned in popularity, but the demand for dancing classes kept growing and Dzung was riding the crest of this wave of enthusiasm, giving private lessons in his studio above the kitchen or in rented halls.

Dzung's habit of taking me to dancing clubs and parties continued long after I stopped taking lessons. He would ring me or sometimes just turn up at my home, and instruct me to change into 'something beautiful' with a full skirt that would swirl and flare. Then off I would go on the back of his motorbike, maybe to a party at the Alliance Française cultural centre, or a special event at the Metropole Hotel to celebrate Bastille Day, or to a university or government office to celebrate the opening of one of Dzung's new dance classes. Apart from the sheer enjoyment of it, Dzung had decided this was a useful marketing strategy to promote his dance classes. As I was usually the only foreigner to be found dancing in these places, I helped draw attention to Dzung, and sometimes we would hit two or three dancing venues in one night, performing just a few dances before heading out into the night again.

According to Dzung, most of the dancers in Hanoi and even the other teachers were unaware of the correct dancing technique, and were often half a century out of date with their steps. As I learnt more from Marion and from studying the dance books, I understood that he was right. But what Vietnamese dancers might lack in knowledge is more than compensated for in the enthusiasm, style and even flamboyance they bring to the art. The stiff self-consciousness often found in Australians when it comes to dancing is nowhere to be found on a Vietnamese dance floor, as couples try to outdo each other with leaps and twirls, hip gyrations and exotic hand and arm movements. Dancing is considered a serious mix of art and exercise. Having some style is well regarded and old and young men will jostle for the privilege of partnering a good dancer, regardless of whether she is twenty-five or sixty-five years. When the disco music comes on, that is the signal for a serious workout, with everyone favouring their own unique exercise routine.

Some dancing clubs still occasionally have live music, but more and more often recorded music is used. Despite government efforts to curb illegal copying of CDs, there is a vast array of pirated music available in Hanoi. Yet the dancing community remains quite conservative in its musical tastes. What this means is that while the crowds might prefer one venue over another, the music played will remain much the same wherever they are. Some of the old favourites are Vietnamese songs, but the modern selection is up-to-date and distinctly MTV in sound. Quickstep and foxtrot music is never played in the clubs because only Dzung and his students know those dances. In fact, a lot of Western-style music is, understandably, unfamiliar to Vietnamese ears, having been banned until relatively recently. This could explain why so often Western tunes have been adapted to an inappropriate dance rhythm, a favourite of mine being the theme from the movie *Exodus* (a biblical epic about the Jews being expelled into the desert) enhanced with a synthetic samba beat. After a while though, you stop caring about or even noticing any shortcomings of the music or the venues. The joyous atmosphere takes over and for an hour or two, just like everyone else there, you forget your cares and lose yourself in the movement and music.

Dzung used to always say to me, and later to Marion, that when the history of ballroom dancing in Vietnam is written, her name and mine would be recorded there, so grateful was he for the opportunity to learn and improve his craft. But of course the real heroes are not a couple of foreigners who dropped by for a short time, but the procession of Vietnamese who kept the love of dancing alight and managed to pass it on to another generation against the odds: Dzung's father, Dzung and his advanced students who are now starting out as teachers themselves, the old couple Ty and Hau. The 'old professor of dancing' died at about ninety years of age. On one of my last visits to the Metal dancing club before leaving Hanoi, I saw the 'young professor of dancing' ('young' only in relation to the 'old' professor) and his wife. He had had a stroke, leaving one side of his body affected by paralysis. Yet he was on the dance floor, only able to shuffle now as his partner whirled and twirled herself around him, but still enjoying the pleasure of the dance as much as he could. Vietnamese may not win any medals in ballroom dancing yet, but as far as the dance of life is concerned, they are champions in knowing how to make the most of enjoying whatever you've got.

Fifty-five hours to Beijing

Australians are used to being a long way from everywhere, even a long way from each other. So it took me some time of living in Hanoi before I realised I was conveniently close to a number of other interesting countries adjoining or near Vietnam. Vientiane in Laos, that smallest and most laid-back of capital cities, is close to Hanoi and therefore handy for a quick break or when a new visa is needed. Cambodia, which also shares a border with Vietnam, is best known in recent times for the murderous evil of Pol Pot, but is also a country with a glorious past when the magnificent temples and monuments of Angkor were constructed one thousand years ago. Entry to Myanmar (Burma) and Nepal, two countries with fascinating ancient cultures, requires a short flight from Hanoi to Bangkok first—a little less convenient perhaps, but still much closer than from Australia. Over the years I took advantage of this proximity. And then there was China, a vast country that shares both a long border with northern Vietnam and a closely interwoven history.

The announcement of the long-awaited opening of the border between China and Vietnam in Lang Son province, north of Hanoi, and the introduction of the Hanoi-to-Beijing rail service caught my attention. This seemed like an adventure too good to miss, so my friend Shuna and I checked out departure times, made our plans and headed off to the travel agent to buy our tickets. Then we hit a snag. We learnt that our Vietnamese visa only allowed arrival and departure by air, and a permit to vary this—so we could leave by train—would take a week, too long for our planned schedule.

Fortunately, Shuna and I had a few years' experience of being entangled in Vietnamese red tape and knew a few tricks of our own. The first rule is never show annoyance or anger, never raise your voice or make demands. We continued to sit at the travel agent's desk and quietly bemoaned the fact that we couldn't go on our trip as planned, that we were very unhappy, that we couldn't go at any other time, all the while making no attempt to leave the office. Finally, we won the psychological battle. Phone calls were made and suddenly our exit visas would be ready in three days, in time for our original departure date.

From Hanoi to the Chinese border takes about six hours in a rattling old Vietnamese train with hard wooden seats and no airconditioning. But the scenery is lovely as it changes from the lush flat rice fields to more mountainous terrain with terraced fields and more varied crops and vegetation. The whole trip from Hanoi to Beijing would take fifty-five hours and we were well prepared. We had brought along plenty of reading material for when we tired of looking out the window, and some snacks, fruit and instant coffee sachets for between meals. We had checked that meals were available on board and that all bedding was supplied, and since the four-berth cabin we had booked was airconditioned, we expected to be comfortable and well rested on our arrival. Most of all, we were excited about the prospect of experiencing an old-fashioned sense of travel, the thrill of taking a long journey, instead of being loaded on and off a plane with its accompanying sense of dislocation and time distortion.

These days it is possible to obtain Chinese currency in Hanoi, but when this train service first began the only place to change money was at the border station. The problem was that the trains from Hanoi crossing into China always arrived late at night, but the money exchange was only open during normal business hours. We weren't too worried about this as we waited in the dark to board the Chinese train at Lang Son station on the border; in Vietnam, US currency is accepted as readily (sometimes more readily) than Vietnamese currency, the *dong*. So we felt sure—mistakenly, as it turned out—that we could use our US dollars on the train. It wasn't until we got onto the Chinese train and tried to buy food that we realised what a serious predicament this was. Here we were in the middle of the night, past the point of any return, still with about fifty hours travel ahead of us and no usable money.

Once we settled into our compartment, the Chinese border police came to check our passports, visas and luggage, then proceeded to confiscate our apples. Ironically, these were imported Chinese apples purchased at a high price in the Hanoi market that morning, but our protests were in vain. It seemed that our food supplies were dwindling before we even got started and our prospects were looking bleak. All we could do was turn back the royal blue velvet pleated bed covers, curl up under our beautifully embroidered quilts on our bunk beds, rest our heads on our white frilled pillows and be gently rocked to sleep in air-conditioned comfort, hoping that some solution would be found the next day.

Early the next morning we arrived at Nanning station. The Vietnamese man who had shared our compartment left the train here to do his trading business, but Morton, a young Danish man who took up the fourth berth, was travelling all the way to Beijing and then on to Ulan Bator in Mongolia to do some research for his doctorate in anthropology, something about the impact of landscape on culture. In the corridor outside our compartment we found a few more foreign tourists milling about uncertainly and discovered that they were in the same predicament as we were with currency. One of them, Raymond, a young Singaporean, could speak Chinese, so he approached the staff on the train and on the station for some advice. They were not particularly helpful, but he understood from them that the train was to wait at this point for about two hours. This, we hoped, would allow us enough time to find a bank or money exchange outside the station since, predictably, the money exchange inside the station did not open until much later.

With some trepidation, our little band of eight hungry travellers, leaving all our luggage on the train, set off to find breakfast and somewhere to change our money, hoping that our Singaporean leader had been given the correct information about the duration of our stop. I could just imagine returning to an empty platform, pockets full of Chinese currency, as our luggage headed for Beijing without us. Outside the station was a small noodle shop open for breakfast. Opposite was a bank. Perfect. But as it was only about 8am by this time, Raymond made an arrangement with the noodle shop owner to supply us with breakfast in exchange for US dollars, which we would change as soon as the bank opened. We fell upon our steaming bowls of noodles hungrily, all the while keeping our eyes on the bank for any signs of opening, and nervously checking our watches and listening for any sounds of a train pulling out.

At last there was some movement inside the bank—morning exercises, it looked like—so we began to make a move. However, by now the noodle shop owner had become a little nervous, uncertain whether he had been duped by a band of foreigners out for a free breakfast. It was therefore decided that I would stay behind as a sort of guarantee of payment. As the time stretched to almost an hour without any sign of my fellow travellers returning, I was starting to imagine a life of imprisonment in a Nanning noodle shop, paying off our breakfast debt and earning enough money to buy a train ticket back to Hanoi by cooking and serving noodles.

Unbeknown to me at the time, the money exchange party had been unsuccessful at the bank opposite. Apparently, US dollars could only be changed at the Bank of China, which this was not. So, trooping after Raymond, the group followed directions to the nearby branch, only to find the bank staff milling about outside, unable to enter because of an electricity failure which prevented the raising of the metal roller security door. No-one knew how long it might take to gain entry and time was passing quickly. Continuing to put their faith in Raymond, the group trotted on to find another bank and, sure enough, another bank was soon encountered. But it was not the Bank of China.

On they went on their quest, lifting the pace as the situation seemed increasingly desperate. Luckily, the next woman Raymond stopped to ask directions of was a street money changer. A few such operators worked on the streets of Hanoi, illegally but more or less overlooked by the police, but it was surprising to find someone willing to flout the law in China. Relieved and anxious to get back to the train, Raymond quickly negotiated an exchange rate. But now the problem was that the money changer only had a limited amount of cash, so my friend Shuna could exchange only US$10 which would have to last the two of us for two days. To make matters worse, because they had walked so far and the time for the train's departure was drawing nearer, everyone had to spend some of this precious Chinese money on a taxi back to the noodle shop to pay our debt and reclaim me, and then make a run for the train.

The rest of the train journey was uneventful. The scenery turned out to be rather disappointing, mainly flat corn fields with few towns or people to be seen. The bathrooms on the train were awful—just a communal wash room with three basins, cold water and no lock on the door, and the toilets weren't cleaned for the duration of the trip. But our compartment was clean and comfortable and we did a lot of sleeping, induced by the rocking of the train, or maybe lack of food. By the end of the trip we were reduced to drinking hot water which was supplied regularly and for free in large red thermos flasks. Not far from Beijing, Shuna and I were about to share our last precious coffee sachet when our Danish companion entered the compartment.

'Mind if I have one of your coffees?' he asked innocently. Politely, we handed him the coffee and proceeded to pour ourselves a cup of hot water each.

'Not having one?' he asked.

'Oh, no,' we chorused, as we inhaled the aroma from his cup. 'We like hot water!'

We were really looking forward to arriving in Beijing; forget about the Great Wall, Tiananmen Square, the Imperial City— we just wanted food and a hot shower. But we still had one more obstacle to overcome. We hadn't booked any accommodation. It had been too hard to arrange that from Hanoi and we felt sure we would find something easily once we arrived.

However, we hadn't counted on arriving with almost no money, just enough for bus fares and not a taxi. And to add a further degree of difficulty to the challenge, we seemed to have arrived at a new central Beijing station which wasn't marked on the maps we were operating from. We were in this enormous station with no idea where to go and only a small booklet from the Chinese embassy in Hanoi with a list of some hotels. Finally, a young woman working in a small kiosk outside the station took pity on us. She spoke and understood a little English, and took us to the bus area (a considerable walk) and put us on a bus that we hoped would take us near some of the hotels listed in the booklet. Strap-hanging in a crowded bus, confused, hungry and surrounded by impassive, expressionless Chinese faces, we began to despair of ever finding a place to stay. Then slowly the atmosphere thawed as we pointed to the advertisement for a hotel in our booklet and mimed our need to be shown where to get off the bus. Amazingly it worked and a few kilometres further along we were directed off the bus where we could see, not far away and to our immeasurable relief, the Chongwenmen Hotel.

There was a vacancy, and although we thought it a bit pricey we checked in, happy to have arrived anywhere, especially as it was fast becoming dark outside. The first thing we did was exchange some money, then we bought some dinner. As we drifted off to sleep that night we still had a rocking sensation after all those hours on board a train. The next morning we set off to find a cheaper hotel, but discovered that we had, in igno-rance, found ourselves a comparatively good deal in a very convenient location right near a subway station and bus stop. So much for the careful planning I used to do to ensure the best possible accommodation before leaving home; 'winging it' and using public transport was clearly the best policy, and we stayed the whole week in our 'suite' with its little sitting room, bedroom and bathroom.

Beijing itself was more wonderful than we imagined. The scale of everything is so large. I knew Tiananmen Square was big, I had seen it on television and heard the statistics, but it wasn't until I started walking across it—walking and walking without ever seeming to reach the other side—that I fully appreciated the size of it. We spent six hours in the Imperial City without seeing everything, another day in the Summer Palace, another day on the Great Wall followed by dinner at a famous multistorey Beijing Duck restaurant which can seat hundreds of diners at a time at round tables big enough for ten or twelve people.

It was a little difficult to get off the beaten tourist track, but we did manage to find some old areas, well behind the main streets, where laneways meandered along and residents could be found relaxing on chairs out on the pavements in the evening or eating in small street restaurants. The style and pace of life here seemed from a different era and it seemed friendlier in these parts, too. Our smiles and nods were returned, and we managed to order a delicious and very cheap meal from a small street eatery by pointing and miming, to the great delight and amusement of the owners.

Back in the main streets and tourist traps, however, the locals seemed less outgoing and friendly than we were used to with Vietnamese, less fun-loving and less enamoured of Westerners, although this is probably an unfair assessment based on our short time in China. There was one incident, though, that made me think again about these differences.

We decided that we could find our own way to the Summer Palace by public bus rather than joining an organised tour. The bus was crowded and we had to sit on tiny plastic stools placed in the centre aisle as all the seats were taken. The conductor collected our fares and although it seemed a little expensive, we were too busy keeping our seating as we swung around corners to worry about it. After some time, a local passenger sitting behind Shuna handed her a small piece of paper on which they had written that we had been charged too much by the conductor. As Shuna was showing this message to me, another passenger caught our eye and pointed to a sign which gave a phone number to call if you had any complaints about the bus service.

By now there was a low hum among some of the passengers, none of them addressing us directly, or the conductor, or even each other, just a general uneasiness. When the conductor came near to collect some more fares from new passengers, we indicated that we were not happy with the cost of our tickets. Immediately, the conductor's face hardened into an impenetrable mask and he refused to acknowledge us. This response, coupled with the unspoken support we felt from many of the passengers, spurred us on. We began to make a big show of writing down the complaints telephone number, of taking the number of the bus, of looking at the conductor for any badges or identification and of looking very stern and serious. Nobody else in the bus would make eye contact with us, the conductor, or each other.

We kept this up until we reached our destination, at which point the conductor, looking extremely guilty, thrust a handful of money at us as we alighted from the bus. It wasn't the full amount we were owed, but it was a significant moral victory and we were pleased. But not half as pleased as our fellow passengers turned out to be. Once we moved away from the bus, they became loquacious and congratulatory, clearly happy and approving of our victory against corruption. Why hadn't they spoken out publicly? Why hadn't they tackled the conductor?

And even more surprising, given their clear desire to stay uninvolved, why had they bothered to alert us at all? We were reassured about the basic goodness of ordinary people, especially the fact that they had sided with a couple of Westerners against one of their own, but a little depressed about the state of a society where people were uncomfortable with speaking out about things they didn't like.

Our holiday was over all too soon. We were glad that we had decided to fly back to Hanoi, not being ready to face another fifty-five hour train journey, although at least we would have had money for food starting from the Beijing end. The only airline operating to Hanoi was China Southern Airlines. I had flown with them in 1994 when I went to Nanjing, and while the service had improved somewhat since then, the food and drinks were still weird and, as if they know this is the case but don't know what to do about it, they keep bringing out small gifts in an attempt to make it up to you. First they handed out a fan, then some socks, and finally in desperation, a key-ring flashlight.

We thought we had booked a direct flight to Hanoi so we went to the international airport check-in section. At first we couldn't find the China Southern check-in at all, then we found a first- and business-class check-in desk, despite the fact that all seats are economy class. From there we were led down some narrow stairs, past toilets and into a large comfortless waiting area with no signs at all. We were worried that we were in the wrong place. Then it became clear; we were in the domestic part of the terminal and our flight was going to stop in Nanning before going on to Hanoi, making it a five-hour flight instead of the short hop we were expecting.

We were not the only passengers who were confused, especially as the information given over the plane's communication system was completely unintelligible. Sitting behind Shuna and me were two Korean businessmen, one very tall and thin, the other very short and round. When we landed at Nanning we had to leave the plane and walk across what looked like a paddock in the middle of the countryside to a small tin shed where we went through some sort of official customs procedure. As we queued up, these Koreans politely asked us if we had arrived in Hanoi and were quite bewildered to discover that we were still in China. For the rest of the trip they stuck close to us and whenever they caught our eyes they would bow and bob and beam at us, clearly impressed that a couple of Western women could tell at a glance the difference between China and Vietnam.

It is often said that the journey and not the destination is important in travel. We had certainly had some interesting journeys on this trip—the fifty-five hour train trip, the five-hour plane trip, and even our short bus trips gave us new insights. I have also heard it said that the greatest pleasure in travelling is in the planning and afterwards in the telling of your adventures, while the actual travel itself is just a bit uncomfortable at the time. Our trip had been uncomfortable at times, but wonderful, too. However, no matter how wonderful the trip away might have been, it was always good to come back to Hanoi. The flight in over the patchwork quilt of rice fields as we began our descent, the familiarity of the small airport, the smells and sounds along the way and finally, the drive across the Red River—gateway to Hanoi and a sight that always took my breath away—made me feel that I had come home. Now we could enjoy the telling of our adventures in comfort.

House-hunting in Hanoi

Finding a suitable place to live in Hanoi is not easy. There is always a huge drawback. Not something minor, like an appalling colour scheme or ugly curtains, a steep ankle-twisting spiral staircase, or no stove—you expect those. But something really major is often wrong, like windowless rooms, the toilet in the kitchen, twelve yapping dogs and a cage of monkeys blocking the way to your front door. Or you might end up with a landlord who thinks he can live in one of your rooms, or his mother lets herself in to keep an eye on things. Or the day after you sign a lease you find that construction is just about to start on a multi-storey building next door.

My first home after leaving the sheltered world of the Post Office Guesthouse was a tiny second-floor flat at the end of a long one-person-wide walkway. The landlord and his family lived on the ground floor and paid careful attention to the maintenance of the building and the comfort of tenants. I felt there was a little too much attention, however, when I returned after a few days away to discover that someone had been going through my computer files while I was gone.

The reason for my departure from my next residence was much more dramatic. I decided that living so close to the landlord was not such a good idea, so instead of a flat, I moved to a house with three floors plus rooftop area—not that I needed a place that large, but this house was back in my old neighbourhood, and because rents in Hanoi had fallen significantly after the Asian economic crisis, it was no more expensive than what I had once paid for just a room. Life there was reasonably comfortable, in a Hanoi way, once I had made the landlord understand that his niece from the countryside couldn't move in with me for a couple of weeks no matter how many spare rooms I might have, and that I didn't want his mother letting herself in and wandering about at will. Then came the fateful night of the big storm.

I was at a friend's house celebrating his wife's birthday when the deluge began, quickly flooding the city. Not wanting to spend the night sharing the floor of my friend's small flat, I decided to brave the weather and accept a lift home with another guest on his motorbike. I had some qualms when we went downstairs and found the front yard flooded to thigh depth, but it was too late to turn back. Off we headed into the night, with rain and wind lashing at us, travelling fast enough to avoid stalling the motor as we drove through a river of water, and trying to keep to the centre of the road where the water was shallowest.

The rain drops were hurting my eyeballs as we sped along and I was terrified, but the relief I felt on reaching my house in one piece quickly turned to dismay when I saw water pouring *out* of my house from under the front door. When I opened the door I was faced with a waterfall cascading down the stairs. Rudimentary plumbing and a blocked drain on the rooftop had created a swimming pool up there, which, on reaching almost shin depth, overflowed into the stairwell. Fortunately the water didn't get into any of the rooms on the two top floors, and after unblocking the drain I was finally able to dry myself off, spread out the sodden contents of my bag to dry out, and go to bed, thinking I had had more than enough excitement for one night.

Suddenly, something woke me out of a sound sleep at about 3am and I could see the outline of a figure in my bedroom, standing near my desk going through the contents of my bag. I know I screamed, but it seemed to me as if the sound I made came from far away. Time stretched. Then the thief sped past me, so close I could have touched him, out the bedroom door and down the stairs, discarding all he had picked up, except money, on the way. I was too terrified to go downstairs to check for a long time, but the stronger fear that maybe my front door was wide open eventually impelled me to go. I saw wet footprints, showing me clearly how the thief had climbed in over a balcony. I also discovered that he had stolen my television set wrapped in my good winter overcoat. I had been a little concerned about security before, but had accepted the landlord's assurances that it wasn't a problem. Now it was definitely a problem and I quickly started looking for a new home.

The next house I moved to was in Quan Su Street in the old quarter, very near all the silk shops. It had three floors and a treacherously narrow, steep spiral staircase. However, it was reasonably comfortable once I got the owner to pull up the dirty carpet, revealing lovely old French floor tiles, and move the kitchen so it was on the same level as the living and dining area. The owner became quite enthusiastic about the improvements so insisted I go with her son to 'shiny furniture street' to buy some ugly, highly lacquered, but functional furniture.

There was, however, the problem of the enormous construction that started next door a month after I moved in. I had been told the land had been vacant for years and would probably never be built on, and even if it was built on it would be a very small building because the land was so small. Wrong, of course. Somehow, the builders managed to create a Taj Mahal on a postage-stamp piece of land, and there were several farce-like scenes with me out on the street in pyjamas at 1am screaming at the builders to turn off the compressor, used to operate the staple gun, that was running under my bedroom window. All to no avail, in a city where there are no rules about noise and appropriate activities for the middle of the night. My landlord was a retired, widowed doctor who spoke French as her second language and only a little English, and we had many misunderstandings. Nevertheless, I probably would have stayed there even longer than my eighteen months just to avoid the trauma of another move, if a friend hadn't left Hanoi for Hong Kong, giving me first refusal on her most desirable residence before her landlord advertised it.

This house, in Phan Boi Chau Street was only small, just the ground floor of an old French villa, but it had a small front courtyard and a verandah for sitting in the sun, and had been renovated properly, even with real paint on the walls and a real kitchen, a washing machine and a dryer. My friend would leave me lots of comfortable furniture, the landlord was a very nice gentleman and the rent was very affordable. Too good to be true? Yes.

The second floor of the house was not owned by my land-lord, a common situation in Vietnam brought about during the time houses were taken away from their rich owners and unre-lated families moved in, or where owners had to sell off part of their title to survive during the hard times. This had not created a problem all the years my friend had lived there, as upstairs was used very little and only during daytime. But shortly after I moved in downstairs, the owner of upstairs died and the relatives who inherited decided to renovate and live there. This meant more than six months of constant building noise day and night, most gratingly the incessant tile cutter. But I loved my new home so much that I was determined I wouldn't be driven from it so easily. Building would have to finish soon, I reasoned, and all would be well again. That was until the family from hell moved in upstairs.

During the day it was relatively quiet, but at about 9pm things would start to warm up and by midnight the cacophony was in full swing. It sounded like a circus going on up there, complete with a herd of elephants and human pyramids falling in a mangled heap. Then they got a dog that barked all night. After that they installed some exercise equipment in their tiny back courtyard, which happened to be right outside my bed-room window. Each morning very early—anything from 5am onwards—and just centimetres from my window were several men puffing, panting and talking loudly as they did chin-ups on a bar and various stretches. Then someone would throw a load of wet washing out of the upstairs window into a tin dish sitting on the concrete near my window and any further thoughts of sleep were well and truly gone.

I complained to my landlord, who complained to the neigh-bours and even to the police, but to no avail. I found their phone number and used to telephone them every time their dog started barking in the middle of the night, but that made no difference. I held on for a year, but in the end I had to give up my dream house and look for somewhere else. The landlord was very understanding. He rented it to some other foreigners, but they couldn't take it and soon moved out. Worried about leaving it empty, the landlord himself moved in, though it was even too noisy for him and his wife. Now, I hear, it has become a café.

Now that I had tasted some Western-style comfort and decor again, I was loath to go back to the spartan living standards of previous places. But it was not easy to find anything suitable, until an agent took me to a house in Au Trieu Street. This quaint old street is near the Notre Dame Cathedral in the centre of Hanoi, very close to Hoan Kiem Lake and to popular cafés and shops, and the house he showed me there was very comfortable and well presented. The owner later told me that he and his wife had studied American home-decorating magazines when they were renovating and decorating. The house had a large living and dining area, study, bathroom and kitchen downstairs, and two bedrooms and a bathroom upstairs. There was also a large upstairs terrace with pot plants and clothes line. It seemed perfect and although it was more expensive than any of my previous places, I decided to treat myself.

Things started going wrong the night before moving, when the upstairs neighbours outdid their earlier efforts with a chorus of barking dogs, yelling humans and assorted bumps and thumps from 2am until dawn. Sleep became impossible and at 6am I staggered to the bathroom to have a shower only to find no water—someone had stolen my water pump during the night! Luckily, there was enough water left in the kettle for a cup of coffee, teeth brushing and a dab around the eyes before the landlord and police arrived to investigate the theft. Moving is generally somewhat stressful, but in Hanoi, oddly enough, it is relatively simple. It is easy to find people to help you; you call a moving van just when you are ready to go, distances across the city are short and all of it is very cheap. Having a fairly minimalist life also helps.

It took a couple of days to get everything put away and to get used to my new house and neighbourhood. During that time I found I was much closer to the cathedral than I had initially thought; in fact, I discovered that a wall of my house was actually the back fence of the church and a large grotto had been constructed on this wall, and further along it was painted a huge mural of the three wise men. Looking over the balustrade of my terrace I could see the star shining in the east, guiding the Magi on camels, and immediately below me were the stones, statues and plants making up the various religious tableaux of the grotto, and a two-storey high cross which lit up at night. Somehow I had managed to miss seeing all this before—I was probably too excited at having real paint on the walls and comfortable furniture.

On the first Friday after I had moved in, I was woken before 6am by loud chanting nearby. I could recognise some of the Vietnamese words being sung: 'father, son and holy ghost'. Intrigued, I went out onto my terrace and found more than one hundred people standing in front of the grotto, singing and looking directly up at me. I wasn't sure if I should give a Papal wave and blessing to the crowd (it was quite a heady feeling looking down upon the worshippers) or whether my appearance in a white nightdress might trigger a series of ghostly sightings. Had they come to welcome me? Or was this going to be a regular feature of Friday mornings from now on? As it turned out, it seemed to be a semi-regular feature—or else I must have slept through it some Friday mornings. It was quite eerie to be woken by a full choir of voices out of nowhere, with no warning, and have them suddenly stop, after almost an hour some days, with no sounds of their coming or going. No footsteps, no speaking; just silence, then full-scale chanting and silence again.

In fact, I didn't really mind this rather interesting facet of life next door to the cathedral. Even the early morning wedding held at the grotto at 6.30am, the bride in full white bridal gown and veil, and kids running everywhere and yelling didn't worry me too much in this city where everyone is up and about early. It was the bells that finally got to me. Three months and I couldn't take any more. I had visions of growing a hump on my back and swinging in the belfry crying, 'the bells, the bells'. First, there was the clock which struck every quarter hour day and (most noticeably) night. But it was the 5am to 6am carillon several times a week that was the real killer, and nothing, not even the double glazing on the bedroom windows, could block it out. Another dream house turned nightmare.

I quickly moved to a small, fairly nondescript apartment for three months while looking for a more permanent place that would serve as residence and bookshop premises. I was relieved to be rid of the ringing and to at last get a reasonably good night's sleep, but at the same time, a little disappointed that I had not stayed long enough to see what the cathedral celebrations for Easter might have been, and that I had lost my group of worshippers.

I had a bookshop in Hanoi

It seemed like a good idea at the time—and it *was* a good idea. But if I had known what was involved, I am not sure I would have embarked on an adventure to open the first English language bookshop in Hanoi.

I had been living in Vietnam for seven years by then and had seen such changes. Back in 1994 when I first arrived, I would use the opportunity of a business trip abroad to go supermarket shopping, taking an empty suitcase and bringing back to Hanoi a supply of washing powder, decent shampoo, cosmetics, tampons, various foods including chocolates and potato crisps, and, most importantly, books. But Vietnam had begun its economic take-off at that time and, to the relief of expatriates and the amazement of locals who clogged up the aisles sight-seeing for the first month of operation, the first supermarket opened in Hanoi in 1995. Initially, the selection of goods offered was eclectic, the supply unreliable and the arrangement on the shelves quirky, if not dangerous. For non-English speakers not familiar with modern products, the difference between air sprays and hair sprays was invisible. For a nation that eats noodles for breakfast, cornflakes were an unknown entity and could be found in any section. And coffee came in little sachets with milk powder and sugar already added.

Nowadays almost anything can be purchased in Hanoi: internationally known cosmetics, French and Australian wines, New Zealand beef, Canadian fox fur coats, Marks & Spencer shoes, Bohemian crystal, the latest Japanese television and DVD technology, Scandinavian cleaning appliances ... the list is endless. But no books!

There are state-owned book shops that cater for Vietnamese customers, with Vietnamese fiction and non-fiction, some foreign language textbooks, a series of English literature classics and sometimes an odd collection of what look like remainders. However, there is a limit to how much Dickens and Hardy and Conrad one can, and wants, to read, and with titles like *Midwifery in 17th century Britain* to tempt you it is hardly worth delving through the rest. These bookshops are rather serious places for students and are nothing like the large Western bookshops we have become used to, with their promotions of latest releases, bestseller lists and reviewed books, all organised according to genres and interests. The locally produced books use poor-quality paper and printing techniques, except for a few coffee-table books produced for the tourist market. Most of the shelf space is devoted to texts for learning English, for passing TOEFL and IELTS exams, writing business English, or texts on business and computers.

Like me, expatriates had to rely on other means of obtaining reading material. You might think that isn't too hard in these days of modern communications and transport. But if you think that, you haven't lived in an emerging communist country where censorship is the norm and there is an active campaign against 'social evils', whatever they might be. Usually everyone carried back as many books as they could each time they went abroad, and hoped no-one would check too carefully at customs. In the early 1990s, books, tapes and computer disks were supposed to be declared and were often submitted to the Ministry of Culture for checking. Over time, the customs checks relaxed and bringing in a few books in your personal luggage (unless they are of an extremely provocative nature, either sexual, political or religious,) became mostly ignored.

These days, if you order a small number of books from online suppliers like Amazon you can often, but not always, receive them. If you have friends or family send them, again you may or may not receive them. It depends. On what? Who knows! Maybe someone whose job it is to check them didn't like them and confiscated them—or maybe they liked them and kept them. Maybe the checker was away and your books got put to one side and forgotten. Or maybe there was a crackdown of some sort and to ensure no blame could be laid, everyone went to ground until the political climate changed again. The chain of cause and effect here is usually too obscure or convoluted for the Western mind to comprehend without guidance.

As tourism has picked up, the number of 'backpacker' cafés offering book exchanges has increased and it is possible to find some good reading there, testament to the literary taste of people visiting Hanoi. But there is usually a lot of dross to sort through and no system in the shelving. And since these establishments are operating in the somewhat 'grey' area of the law and in the tough competitive business environment where small enterprises regularly fail, they cannot necessarily be relied on.

This then was the backdrop to my epiphany. Why didn't I open a bookshop in Hanoi for the foreigners living here? All booklovers, it seems, harbour a fantasy about running a bookshop some day. Here was my chance to make that dream come true, and in an undreamed of exotic location. And if any further inducement was needed, I would have that highly prized but elusive business condition: a virtual monopoly.

Before I completely committed to this bright idea I had a little trial run. Over the years I had collected not only my own books, but also books from friends who had returned home. As I was about to move house again and was tired of carrying this load with me I decided to have a street stall outside my place one Sunday morning. I sent out a few emails to various locals and pasted a few flyers on noticeboards around town. Before the sale day I had one bulk purchase for about one-third of my stock. And the rest flew off the tables in about ninety minutes on the day of the sale. My first group of customers arrived before the starting time of 10am. They apologised for being early but said they hadn't been able to contain their excitement since they saw the notice. Here then was proof that there was a need, and I also now had a feel for the type of books people liked.

And so it was with fearless optimism, buoyed by the resounding success of my little sale, that I took the first fateful step to becoming the first-ever owner of an English language bookshop in Hanoi. Of course I knew it wouldn't be easy; seven years living and working in this city had taught me that, at least. Part of the attraction—and I guess I use the word attraction in the same sense as a cobra mesmerising its prey—was that you couldn't predict the exact form the difficulty would take. I also knew I wouldn't be able to do it alone. I needed a Vietnamese partner to help me chart a course and interpret not just language but, more importantly, meaning.

Vietnam wants foreign investment, but it wants it, rightly enough, on its own terms. And it really isn't interested in small investors. Large, well-known Western or Japanese companies with big budgets and high technology are wooed in the hope of a joint-venture deal which will bring in lots of foreign currency and perks. In the years since the introduction of the open door policy in 1986, the government has been working on foreign investment laws, but the focus naturally has been on these big benefit deals. Individuals like me, wanting to invest in small enterprises, were of no real interest economically to the government. The numerous small restaurants, travel agencies, training and consulting establishments, fashion shops and so on in town, which were inspired, backed and run by foreigners, were usually registered as owned by Vietnamese to simplify things. But books were in a different category altogether since they were considered 'cultural items', and were therefore politically sensitive.

Only Vietnamese citizens could own a bookshop in Vietnam and only, we were told, after they had undertaken a training course at the Culture University. I had already decided to take my young friend Minh, whom I had known for more than a year, as my new partner. He had recently finished his university degree and hadn't yet found a job, so this arrangement seemed mutually beneficial. I thought it should be a simple step for him to undertake the required training, but I was wrong to suppose that.

Misinformation abounds in Vietnam, and because laws and regulations are emerging, changing or sometimes non-existent and almost never in writing in any accessible form, the character and position of the person who gives you information is of vital importance. Getting hold of the right person can be quite a task. This is where the bureaucratic merry-go-round began. Was there such a course for bookshop owners? Opinions varied. Minh finally tracked down the head of the university department responsible for running these courses and learnt that one would be held soon, but no-one could say exactly when it would start and whether it would run for one month or three. He left his name on a list to be contacted when there were enough names to hold a class. He rang regularly to check on progress. Then one day he was told that enrolment would take place the following week. He arrived with his fees on the appointed day, ready to enrol, only to find the entire staff of the department missing. He waited. He came back after lunch; in the afternoon he rang the director at home, only to be told by her daughter that she was sleeping! He tried again the next day and managed to give his fees to the only person he could find. Not surprisingly, he was later advised that there were not enough people enrolled to hold a class.

In the end there was no class and I doubt there has ever been a class, maybe just the payment of class fees and the issuing of a certificate of attendance. And there was further talk that maybe the rules had been changed and it was no longer necessary to even say you had attended such a class. And so the issue that had been of primary importance to our getting started had melted away, leaving a very unfinished feel to the episode.

It had become clear by this time that if I was committed to going ahead with this plan I had to take that leap of faith and just do it, in the same way that you cross the roads in Vietnam. Putting aside all your childhood training, you have to stride out into the traffic and keep going at a regular, confident pace, step by step, looking straight ahead, hoping that the oncoming traffic will weave around you, washing you up unscathed on the other side. The business equivalent was to do little business planning beyond some scribblings which calculated that if one in five of the estimated English-reading expat population of Hanoi bought one book a month we could cover overheads. How we could get the books, what rules and regulations and charges there might be we didn't know exactly, but if we waited until we had the full picture we would never get started because something would always be changing.

The next step to investigate was importation procedures and this is when we learnt that only the state-owned book companies could import foreign books into Vietnam. Once, I would have considered that to be the end of my dream: mission impossible. But I had learnt that 'no' doesn't mean 'no', it just means you have to 'find the way', as the Vietnamese will tell you. Finding the way in this case meant finding someone who worked for a state-owned company who was prepared to have a 'relationship' with us and assist in the importation process. Using our network of trusted contacts we finally found someone to help us, Mr Hung. But like a Chinese whisper that can end up quite a different message by the time the last person receives it, the guarantee of trustworthiness and reliability diminishes as the distance between first and last contact increases. Mr Hung assured us that he was ready, willing and able to help and I was reassured that it was quite legal. As time went on and Mr Hung became less ready and willing, I began to doubt whether or not he actually was able. Even today I am not exactly sure, but I suspect we were operating in a legal area which was towards the darker shade of gray.

One of the first problems encountered was when I wanted to import a few hundred used books to start off a second-hand collection. In Vietnam you are not allowed to import secondhand anything it seems. This principle seems to have originated from feelings of pride, that Vietnamese people deserve to have the latest and newest of everything, and from bad past experiences when some rather shady deals were done in joint ventures where old machinery and technology was passed off and valued as new. The fact that books were still valuable, old or new, was not considered. Nevertheless, Mr Hung agreed that we should try since it wasn't all that clear and he had the authority to arrange it—or so he said. I tried importing a few boxes on my own, sent by my brother in Australia, without Mr Hung's help, and owing to a good relationship with the customs people at the post office, I managed to get them through at just a small customs charge. But the message was clear that I couldn't expect to do it too often or with too many books, especially with titles like Peter Goldsworthy's *Honk if you are Jesus,* which caused the customs officer to wag her finger at me and say 'no', believing it to be a religious tract, I suppose.

New books required very different procedures and while the rules were clear, their execution wasn't always transparent. As the process became murkier and Mr Hung's requirements became greater, and his availability less, we began to fear the long-term viability of this relationship. So it was back to the contact network to see if we could find an alternative partner to import our supplies. After sensitive negotiations we managed to find a new company to help us, one where the commitment and responsibilities were clear and so were the costs of their service.

The process went like this: I had to provide a list, translated into Vietnamese, of the book titles I wanted to import, to the Ministry of Culture. This sounds reasonable. Spare a thought, however, for Minh, who had to translate the titles, especially when you know that these translations will be taken quite literally and could result in the book being banned. Sensitive translation was required. How do you translate, for example,

A clockwork orange and make any sense out of it for the men in 'cultural control'? After I had explained the meaning of 'impotent' to Minh, so he could translate the title *In search of an impotent man*, we decided to fudge and claim a misreading, converting it to *In search of an important man*, although that too could be liable to political or religious interpretation. This was not paranoia on our parts. In one of our submissions we had the following titles rejected: *The poisonwood bible*, no doubt mistakenly believed to be a religious tract, likewise *The buddha of suburbia*; *When I was five I killed myself* (perhaps they thought it advocated suicide); the thriller, *The church of the dead girls*—religion and killing no less; *The ghost road*, probably seen as superstitious; and *As we lay bare*, clearly pornographic!

Once we had our list approved and the licence to import these books, I could then notify the book suppliers to send the amended order. I had expected there would be challenges at the Vietnam end of things, but I hadn't realised how difficult it would be to find suppliers. It seemed that anything a little out of the ordinary, like sending books to Vietnam, was beyond most suppliers. After lots of unanswered emails and calls for help I finally found a few Australian publishers willing to supply me, at no risk to them since I was paying up front. If the books didn't make it, it was my pocket that would be empty.

There was a lot of tension both while waiting for news that an order worth thousands of dollars had left Australia, and then on checking on its arrival. Once it arrived at the airport in Hanoi, the customs people would check that the titles of the books sent matched those listed on the licence. Oh, and we had to pay the checkers to do that! Then the state-owned book company that was importing for us was took delivery of the books and arranged for the agents from the Ministry of Culture and from the police to check all the books, and again we had to pay them for this 'service'. It could take several days and I don't know what they expected to find. But they did confiscate some books.

One time, the books sat for so long at the airport because of problems with documents that rats ate through the boxes and began munching on the books; Graham Greene's *The end of the affair* and Philip Roth's *American pastoral* had to be thrown away, and others with nibbles and teeth marks sold off cheaply. As we became a bit more experienced, and Minh was able to build a relationship with the checkers, he could be present at the inspections and he found that the books confiscated usually had what the inspectors considered risqué covers, a threat to society by promoting 'social evils'. This was an expensive problem if we lost too many books and one that we couldn't control, since most of the time we didn't know what was going to be on the cover. So Minh came up with the bright idea of supplying the inspectors with a can of spray paint so they could cover any offending art work. Not only did this save me losing money, it actually encouraged sales as everyone wanted a copy of a book that had been sprayed for their protection by Cultural Control! Quite a talking point, in fact. And quite ludicrous. I am sure Margaret Atwood would be surprised to know that one of her paperbacks was given the spray treatment—there were nude statues depicted on the cover. *La Cucina*, a book based around Italian cooking, had a naked back, not even a photograph, sprayed. I hate to think what they would have done to art books!

At the same time we were learning about how to get the books, we were also finding and preparing a shop. Real estate is expensive in Hanoi and cannot be owned by foreigners. Places that foreigners are allowed to rent are regulated by the government and are quite expensive, although as the supply has increased with new buildings and the number of foreigners decreased with the fall in investment projects, rents have dropped considerably. When I first arrived in Hanoi and stayed at the Post Office Guesthouse, I paid US$660 per month for a room with bathroom but no kitchen, no heating and very basic furniture. By 2001 I could rent a three-storey building unfurnished but suitable to use as bookshop and residence for the same amount. The owner lamented as we signed the lease agreement that back in 1996 she was getting more than US$2000 per month rent for it.

The building was not in a mid-city, central tourist area, where rents were out of our price range, but I guessed that it wouldn't take long for word of our location to pass around the expat community. The other advantage was that I had a reasonable place to live at no extra cost and with the luxury of having all those books nearby; like Scrooge McDuck from my childhood comic reading, who used to dive into his swimming pool full of money and splash it over himself, I could come downstairs and play with my books, dipping into them or devouring them at will.

Finding the right premises was just the beginning. Then we had to fit it out, which involved painting, new lighting, repairing airconditioners, having shelves, bookends and counters made and buying chairs, computers, a music system. Initially we tried to find someone to design and arrange everything, but found there was no understanding of what we wanted for a Western-style bookshop. Design sketches were submitted to us that bore no relationship to the space in which we were operating, or to practical, functional considerations. There were drawings of glass-fronted bookcases looking like they were destined for some baronial mansion of the 19th century, clearly copied from some reference source they had found. A more contemporary design had shelves hinged to the wall so they could swing out. When I questioned the designer about the practical nature of this and how they could support the weight of a few hundred books, a certain vagueness appeared.

After several attempts to inject practical considerations and have prospective designers take account of the brief they were given and not some flight of fancy they might have gleaned from an old Russian architectural text, Minh and I decided to do the design ourselves, keeping it simple and elegant. But we didn't want to completely discourage these young entrepreneurs when they failed to satisfy us. When you are a foreigner living in a developing country, especially one with a history like Vietnam, there is a feeling of responsibility to help in some way, whether it be to help someone improve their English language skills, to help them get a better education or job, to guide them or introduce new ideas and ways of thinking and doing. So we engaged them to manage the construction of the shelves, counters and facade which we designed while we found painters, electricians and went shopping for other supplies ourselves.

It was the usual list of horror stories you expect with building and decorating, with a few extra Vietnamese twists, like the police impounding all the shelves for some days because the makers had tried to save a little money by transporting them illegally on a convoy of cyclos instead of renting a small truck. In the process of off-loading at the police station, paintwork was scratched and so when eventually released after some negotiation and payment, they had to be touched up and repaired. Then there were the daredevil metal workers who welded the new facade on to the front of the building without using any protection or safety procedures. Sparks went shooting towards overhead electricity wires and cascading onto the footpath and parked motorbikes, as the workers dangled precariously from a balcony. I became the centre of a piece of street theatre as I tried to explain, using limited Vietnamese and mime interspersed with loud shouting in English, the need for priming raw metal surfaces before applying enamel paint. The so-called painters watched me impassively but the customers at the nearby crowded noodle stall clearly enjoyed the spectacle.

Other things went wrong, too. The metal bookends we had ordered had been stacked together before the paint was dry and so when prised apart, the paint came off. And we had taken great care designing planter boxes to sit outside and then finding someone to make them to our specifications. When we went to collect them, we found the police had completely razed the area where these workers plied their trade and there was no sign of our planter boxes or the person we had paid to make them. As a substitute we bought large ceramic pots and filled them with attractive shrubs; they lasted less than twelve hours before being stolen.

It was an exhausting month and tempers were frayed, and I was tired of hearing 'but this is Vietnam' as an excuse for shoddy work and people not turning up. However, in the end we had a bookshop that looked reasonable, even the trompe l'oeil we had painted on the front of the building to look like a bookcase wasn't too bad—not quite as I'd imagined but okay nevertheless.

Then on opening day, the heavens decided to open and the road in front of our shop became a small river. Every time a car or bike drove carefully by, small waves would lap at the front door. Our first customers arrived soaked to the skin. The rain kept up for another couple of days and large parts of Hanoi were under water. Our grand opening was a bit of a wash-out.

However, undaunted, grateful customers with raincoats and umbrellas waded and pedalled there and, thankfully, bought our books. Praise came thick and fast: 'Bless you for doing this,' said one satisfied bibliophile. 'The best bookshop in South-East Asia apart from Singapore,' said another. 'One of the best bookshops in the world!' claimed another, causing me to wonder where exactly he had been. All the trials and tribulations of setting up, the hassles with getting books faded away as the dream came to fruition. We had actually opened the first English language bookshop in Hanoi. The trick now was to keep it open!

In addition to attracting customers and making a profit, this meant not provoking authorities and keeping everyone on-side. I wanted to operate as close to the letter of the law as possible but it was often hard to do. I had to force payments onto the tax department. Every other shop keeper in the street would run away when the tax men came; I would chase the tax men, trying to get them to come into my shop. Seems they couldn't speak English and were too shy to deal with me. The local police were also too shy, but still managed to communicate the message that 'security payments' were appropriate. We also didn't want to make too much of an advertising splash in case it was misinterpreted as trying to corrupt the Vietnamese by luring them into our shop to read 'Western propaganda'. There is considerable tolerance for Westerners in Vietnam these days, provided they keep their 'social evils' within their own groups, and so I advertised in places foreigners frequented, in magazines they read, and relied on the very effective expat grapevine for word to pass around.

The internal security police were another story, however. Most of the time I lived in Vietnam I was able to forget that all foreigners were under some level of scrutiny, although once in a while I would be brought up short with a reminder: with stories, for example, that a journalist had been expelled just before the National Party Congress, that an American woman had her visa revoked for bringing in provocative political literature, that the person who organised a 'gay bash' at the Press Club was asked to leave. Vietnamese friends would remind me to be careful what I said on the phone and wrote in faxes and, later when connected, in emails. Whenever you moved to new accommodation or received a visa extension every six months, you had to report to the police, and every organisation that employed foreigners had people who reported on their activities to the authorities. But it didn't feel oppressive, and provided you weren't engaging in activities that threatened the state, you were usually left alone. On the positive side, you always felt physically safe and could walk almost anywhere at any time unmolested. And you always felt that while the police may be able to collect all sorts of information on you, their capacity for storing and retrieving it seemed comfortingly inadequate.

The ploy of the shop being registered in Minh's name did not fool the security police for a minute, and they kept in constant contact with him. Initially they told him not to tell me of their interest, then after we had been open a few weeks they wanted to arrange a meeting with me. The questions they asked Minh were whether I knew writers, whether I was writing anything myself, who I mixed with, why I was doing this.

When I met with them, however, it seemed such issues were furthest from their mind. The first meeting was arranged to take place in a tea shop and the conversation followed the pattern of all polite conversation in Vietnam between Vietnamese and foreigners: what did I feel about Vietnam and Vietnamese people, how did I enjoy living there, what did I think about future foreign investment in their country? I had gone armed with an array of legal documents but they waved them away, saying this was an informal chat. I started to tell them about some of the activities I had participated in while living there like ballroom dancing, and where I had lived, but they quickly brushed that aside and said they knew all that. After forty minutes the interview ended and I left puzzled by what they had gained. Two days later they rang Minh to ask him what I had thought of the meeting! Seems the East and West are equally inscrutable to each other!

I had a few Vietnamese customers; some, I suspect, were checking up for the police, looking for unsuitable books. Not that there was a list of banned books, or one that I could discover at least, but I was careful about what I ordered and self-censored, avoiding any books written by overseas Vietnamese, any books written about Vietnam and its leaders, and anything that might be misinterpreted. Other Vietnamese customers had lived overseas or studied English literature, but usually the prices (other than for some secondhand copies) were too high for them. I discovered that, in general, English literature of the 20th century was unknown to most Vietnamese, and was not taught in their universities. One young woman made it clear she didn't think it much of a bookshop when I informed her that I had no books by Jane Austen. 'But she's a very famous writer!' she told me.

One day a middle-aged Vietnamese man with a limp came in and began flicking through the pages of various books, reading aloud a word here and there. When asked if he needed help he answered, 'Looking, looking'. He then launched into a long monologue in broken English interspersed with what sounded like German, from which I gleaned he had once studied in Stuttgart in Germany. For some reason he took a shine to me and would come to the shop regularly, raving on about Stuttgart and 'looking, looking'. Sometimes he would come by bicycle, other times on a motorbike. If there were other customers he could be quite a nuisance, trying to speak to them in German, pushing certain books onto them and telling them his Stuttgart story. He was very excited when he noticed a Stuart Little book in the children's section, pointing out that it almost spelled Stuttgart. Then he started bringing me cakes. I began to dread his visits and adopted a stern attitude and herded him quickly out the door. But I did give him full marks for trying when he arrived dressed up one afternoon and after nervously pacing around the shop invited me to have dinner with him. I declined, but, undeterred, as he was walking backwards towards the door he said, 'Perhaps a little wine?'

'No, thank you,' I replied.

'Maybe some water?' he asked as he bumped into the door-frame and tripped backwards out the door.

I enjoyed the passing parade of customers and learning about the reading tastes of my regulars; some would linger and we would discuss favourite books and new discoveries. As a book-loving teenager I used to fantasise about being accidentally locked in a bookshop. Now at the close of business each day I was locking myself in my own bookshop, a dream come true. However, there is always a danger of dreams slipping into nightmares and Hanoi has any number of monsters lurking in the shadows waiting to pounce, whether in the guise of new regulations and red tape, over-zealous officials or even acts of God. Having got this far, the challenge now was to keep the dream alive and viable.

I eventually decided to go back to Australia, eight years in Vietnam suddenly seeming like a long time. When that time came, I mentioned this decision to a customer with whom I had become very friendly. She was an Australian woman looking for a new adventure to take her out of Canberra. And so she bought my bookshop and is living there happily ever after—I hope!

The rat

I had opened my bookshop, a desperate act to ensure some decent reading material in a place where you had to bring enough books with you, or beg and borrow from other expatriates, hoping they shared your taste. The pains and traumas of setting up The Bookworm, as we eventually named it, and getting the first order of books through customs and cultural control were beginning to fade as the routine of running the bookshop got going, and I was getting to know my neighbours and the pattern of daily life in my new street.

Ngo Van So Street is only a small street that can be easily overlooked, but is known by most foreigners living in Hanoi since it boasts a rather nice restaurant, Le Tonkin, and, situated on the corner, is the long-established Western Canned Food Store, well patronised by the expatriate community. There were a few foreigners living in the street, too, renting some nice old French villas, but I was the only foreigner operating a business there and so aroused a lot of curiosity among the locals. Everyone had watched with great interest as I fitted out the shop and moved in, and once I opened for business they watched my daily routine, noticeably surprised to see me sweep the shop and pavement each day instead of having a Vietnamese assistant do it for me. First thing, every few days, I would buy fresh flowers from the passing flower sellers. Later in the day I would sometimes buy a fresh bread roll from the roving bread sellers, or else I'd arrange for the little lunchtime eating stall around the corner to bring me a tray with rice, meat, vegetables, maybe an egg, soup and a small bottle of Coke. Over time, familiarity grew and I began to feel part of our small community and less of a novelty show.

To Vietnamese, Ngo Van So Street is best known for its many small carpet shops and before Tet each year, when everyone is decorating their home, the street is abuzz with activity. Because each shop was minute, the roadway became the only place to measure and cut large lengths of carpet, and since it was usually free from garbage in front of my shop and reasonably flat and level, it wasn't unusual to see huge rolls of red or other coloured carpet being unrolled there and traffic diverted. On one side of my building was the office for a Vietnamese export company and I had a running battle with the staff there, who insisted on parking their motorbikes on the footpath, taking up the whole of my frontage and blocking my front door. Each day I would have to ask them to move their bikes, and if my Vietnamese partner was around he would just move the bikes out onto the roadway after several months of frustration. On the other side, was housing for street children. Things sometimes got a bit rowdy there, especially if they were left unsupervised at night, but most of the time I think they were too tired and hungry to do much more than sleep after a hard day of trying to eke out a living, polishing shoes on the streets of the city.

Opposite was Le Tonkin with its full-time staff out the front to park and mind patrons' and staff motorbikes and bicycles. This was a boring job but these young men managed to entertain themselves, and sometimes the street, with their antics, kicking a shuttlecock, laughing and joking, accidentally knocking over a row of bikes, making purchases from passing sellers, teasing the girls and lots of eating. Next to the restaurant, at the head of a small laneway, was an outdoor noodle stall run by an old couple. I would hear them sweeping the area and setting up at about 4.30am every morning. Tables and stools were carried down the laneway from their home, the blue plastic awning hung up, bowls and chopsticks laid out, the cauldron heated and hundreds of bowls of *pho* were dispensed for breakfast and early lunch. After that it became a café until about 5pm when they would pack up for the day.

From the same laneway, but a bit later in the morning—usually around 7am—came the young woman who sold cooked fertilised duck eggs containing an embryo, a favourite breakfast delicacy among Vietnamese. Always neat, clean and carefully made up, she sold up to thirty eggs each day. She had just a small plastic table and a few stools, and would change her position according to the weather and any obstructions in the street, but most days she would set up outside or next to my shop. She would leave mid-morning and her position would be taken by another young woman who carried her fried tofu restaurant on her shoulder pole, in one basket the small coke fire, usually with the small pan frying away as she walked, and in the other a few small plastic stools for customers, chopsticks and paper napkins. Pavements are very much public property in Vietnam. A street masseur used to operate from about 8pm to midnight outside one house I lived in, rolling out his straw mat for customers and ringing my doorbell to ask me to turn on my outside light so he could read between customers. I didn't mind these women setting up their portable restaurants outside my shop so long as they didn't take up too much room, and they always swept up before they went, using a communal broom I used to leave near the doorway.

One morning, not long after I had moved there, I came downstairs to open the shop and was met by a dreadful smell. The duck egg woman came rushing over to me holding her nose and pointing to where the metal security grille doors at the front of the shop slid into the wall cavity. Before then we had only exchanged smiles and nods, but I was aware that she had some disability which left her unable to speak and able to communicate only by grunts and gesticulation. Nevertheless, the meaning was very clear in this case and she had moved her table and stools a bit further away to avoid the stench.

By this time the motorbike minder from the restaurant across the road wandered over to check out the situation and get in on the act. 'A rat!' he said conclusively, and went off to find a torch. Even the weak beam his torch produced was enough to confirm this conclusion—we could only see its tail, which was as thick as a piece of rope! The duck egg woman and I couldn't go near or even look at it.

By now there was a lot of interest in the situation. The motorbike minder was joined by a cyclo driver who lived a few doors away and who recommended buying spray to cover the smell. I gave him some money and he went off somewhere and returned with a pump spray called Pari, which turned out to have an aroma that you *know* is covering up something dead and rotten.

We all knew that there was only one thing to do: get rid of

the body. But how, and more importantly, who? The motorbike minder knew, without anyone saying anything, that it had to be him. He went across to the restaurant to get one of their green cotton serviettes and tied it around his face, but even then the smell overwhelmed him and he had to keep rushing to the gutter to cough and spit. He put a large plastic bag over his hand and reached into the cavity, and after several attempts pulled out an enormous dead rat the size of a small dog. He ran up the road with it and threw it in the gutter, away from my shop and his restaurant. We all felt sick.

My Vietnamese business partner arrived at the shop a couple of hours after all the excitement had died down. Before he could get off his bike, the duck egg woman raced over to him and started to communicate the story to him, much to his amusement. I asked him what I should give the motorbike minder to reward him and was told a pack of cigarettes. It didn't seem nearly enough—I would have given my kingdom a few hours before! But my hero seemed delighted with this compensation.

I was a bit worried about the fact that we had just left the dead rat in the gutter, but no-one else was and I didn't know how to dispose of it in a more responsible way. But retribution was at hand. That afternoon there was a torrential downpour and, as usual, Ngo Van So Street quickly flooded. Standing in my doorway watching the rising water I was horrified to see the now bloated rat floating down the small river that was forming in my street and heading right towards me! As I stood transfixed, my personal rat catcher, who must have spotted it at the same time, leapt into action. Quickly wading across the road, he grabbed my communal broom and just before it landed at my feet, he swept the rat downstream, grinning at me all the while.

I spent the next few days trying to wash away the smell of the Pari spray. But the motorbike minder, the cyclo driver, the duck egg woman and I had bonded and from that time on exchanged special smiles, recalling our traumatic moments with the rat.

The international film festival, Hanoi style

Adjusting to expatriate life in Hanoi in the 1990s meant learning to live without television and films. Of course, those expats living in foreign embassy compounds usually had access to satellite television and video collections, but the rest of us had to learn how to entertain ourselves. Sometimes foreign embassies or foreign companies would organise special cultural exchange concerts, bringing in international artists: a cellist from Russia, a pianist from China, a harpist from Cuba, a singer from Korea. Unfortunately, Hanoi's only English language newspaper, the *Vietnam News,* had the exasperating habit of omitting a vital piece of information, such as the date or venue of the performance, or would publish full details of the concert the day after the artist had gone home. Once, I went to great lengths to track down a ticket, only to find when I turned up for the performance that the printed date was incorrect and the concert had been held the previous night. What all this confusion meant was that regardless of what the performance turned out like, you felt you had won by merely being there!

There were a number of old dilapidated cinemas around Hanoi, showing local and Chinese films which even the locals were not interested in, preferring to rent videos. And then Fansland opened. It began in a small way with a local Vietnamese film enthusiast occasionally showing his private collection of videos publicly for a small fee. Entertainment-starved expats and local Vietnamese wanting to hear foreign languages made up the first small audiences, but as word spread and its popularity grew, Fansland moved to a small hall in Ly Thuong Kiet Street and a thriving business was established.

The screen at Fansland was about the same size as that on a plane—and the quality of the picture and sound was also about the same. The seating, fixed rows of hard wooden lift-up seats, was distinctly uncomfortable, and during summer, as the temperature soared in the unairconditioned hall, the varnish on the seats began to melt and you found yourself literally stuck to your seat. Nevertheless, crowds queued for tickets and were sometimes turned away when popular new films were shown. It was certainly the test of a good film if you could endure the discomforts.

As welcome as Fansland was at that time, there were only a limited number of times you could watch *Four Weddings and a Funeral*, *Forrest Gump*, and *The English Patient*, enjoyable as they might have been the first or even second time around. And so the announcement that an international film festival would come to Hanoi each year was met with great anticipation and excitement. But old habits die hard, and even though we were expecting it and watching for it, it was always difficult to find out exactly when the festival would start and what was on the program. Usually it had been running for two or three days before *Vietnam News* got around to reporting it. Programs seemed impossible to find, although at the end of the festival when everything was over, great piles of them appeared all over town.

Over the years, I had managed to make it to a few of these films, usually thanks to friends who worked in or had a contact in the participating embassies bringing me a ticket. In 2001 I was determined that I would be prepared this time, yet despite my best efforts, the New Zealand and Danish offerings were over before I knew the festival had even started. The next night I set off to see the French film but was turned away because I didn't have a ticket. In the past, you could turn up at the theatre, and if there were any spare seats once the film started, the organisers would let you in. But in 2001 the event was held just a few weeks after the September terrorist attacks in the United States, and Hanoi was on high alert with armed guards wearing bullet-proof vests posted all around the city, including outside the film festival cinema hall.

With still another week of films to go, I realised that if I wanted to see any films I would have to get tickets before the event, and this proved quite an exhausting quest. No-one had come up with the idea that there should be a central place for obtaining tickets. Instead, you had to go in person to each embassy that had a film in the festival and ask for a ticket. I decided to hire a motorbike taxi for the afternoon and do the rounds of the embassies in one afternoon.

The British, Dutch, Japanese and Israeli embassies had no tickets left by the time I got there. At the Israeli embassy there were armed guards everywhere and when I buzzed the main gate a voice shouted through a speaker, 'Stand back from the gate, stand back from the gate!' The official who then came out to see me (by now I was standing almost on the roadway in my efforts to avoid being shot for standing too close to the gate) asked if I was Jewish or an Israeli. After telling him I wasn't, he went back inside and eventually sent someone else to tell me there were no tickets left. I decided by this time that I wasn't strong enough to face the Germans, the last embassy on my list, so my afternoon had netted me only four tickets for films from Finland, Korea, China and Spain—an eclectic mix.

Unfortunately, the difficulty of obtaining tickets was in no way related to the quality of the films being shown. In the early days of the festival, the issue of copyright was ignored and current release award-winning movies were shown. By 2001, however, the Vietnamese were trying very hard to be seen to crack down on pirated and illegal CDs and films to satisfy the US trading requirements. So, rather than being a showcase for the latest and best in cinema, the festival ended up an odd assortment of whatever the embassies could come up with from their country that was cheap and available. The Spanish offering was ninety minutes of 'authentic' flamenco dance and music with no dialogue, which wore a little thin after about twenty minutes. After watching Finland's contribution I had to read the program synopsis to check what it had been about. All those long winters take their toll, I think! *Love Bakery* was a South Korean film trying to look like a Hollywood romantic comedy. The Koreans in the audience clearly loved it, applauding enthusiastically at the end, while most Westerners were merely bemused by the overacting and corny plot.

However, for me it was the Chinese offering that stole the show. *Mr Chairman of the Women's Association* was about a doltish husband who was sent in place of his wife to represent the village at the district meeting of Women's Associations. In trying to big-note himself, he described to the committee a non-existent program of village activities, including document study, family planning and environmental classes. The leaders were so impressed that they made a decision to go to the village to see for themselves. All the inhabitants then had to rally to try to turn these claims into a reality before the visit. In the end the officials never made it, but no-one in the village seemed to mind, and in a musical finale to rival Hollywood we saw old and young villagers dancing around Mr and Mrs Chairman of the Women's Association, singing their newly written family planning song about how there are already too many people on earth and so they should raise more pigs and not more children!

I don't know how old the film was, but the quality was dreadful and colouring bizarre, like very early Technicolor with unnatural iridescent blobs of purple and red depicting autumn colours of the countryside and highly rouged cheeks and lips. And there was one final touch that completed the absurdity for me: for some reason the Chinese official at the embassy had given me a ticket for the Vietnamese-dubbed version, although how he could have missed the blue eyes and Australian accent and mistaken me for a Vietnamese is a mystery. Maybe they had run out of tickets for the foreign version and he gave me his rather than disappoint me?

What this meant was that as well as having the original Chinese dialogue and very poorly translated English subtitles (which added yet another element of humour) I had to try to block out the Vietnamese language dubbing. This was not professional dubbing, pre-recorded as part of the soundtrack. Rather, it consisted of a woman sitting at the back of the room with a microphone, speaking all the parts with no expression whatsoever! Interestingly, I could actually ignore it after a while, only to be reminded when there were odd microphone noises or occasionally a protracted period of silence, causing me to wonder whether she had gone off to the toilet, lost her place, knocked off work or given up because the plot was too silly and obvious. I was sitting in the front row because my experience has always been that just as the lights dim in the theatre, the entire team of Harlem Globetrotters dashes in and sits in front of me, so it wasn't until the end of the film when I got up to leave that I realised I was the only non-Asian in the audience.

Back in Sydney there are 'real' film festivals and it is so easy to get tickets and programs, but somehow the excitement and anticipation aren't there for me. Sure, the seats are comfortable, the quality of the sound and picture good, the films themselves worthy, award-winning or groundbreaking. So maybe the difference is that in Australia we are sated with so many stimuli, with so many choices. Or maybe it is to do with the setting. It is always a little disorienting to come out of the dark of a cinema and back to everyday reality in the streets. But after losing yourself in some British period piece, or even an American or Australian contemporary film, and then to plunge into the bustling noisy streets of downtown Hanoi has quite a surreal feeling. Or perhaps the difference is just that when you live in an exotic place like Hanoi, everything becomes interesting and every day is an adventure.

The owl

I was desperate to escape the city's oppressive midsummer heat and the feeling of too many cars and too many people. A trip to the coast was too far for just a day, so my friend and business partner Minh suggested we go by motorbike to Sui Hai, about eighty kilometres from Hanoi, where there is a large artificial lake which is isolated enough to attract only a few visitors. Armed with a picnic lunch, towels and swimming costumes we set off early to avoid the searing sun. Sui Hai was certainly no Bondi Beach, but the water was clean and we enjoyed a relaxing day of eating, lazing under a tree and dipping in and out of refreshing water until the local buffalo chased us away when they arrived for their afternoon ablutions.

Heading back to Hanoi in the lengthening afternoon shadows, I needed a cold drink and asked Minh to stop at the next drink stall he saw along the roadside. As we walked over to the stall we noticed some young boys gathered nearby in a tight group, talking very excitedly. Minh's curiosity got the better of him and, leaving me to my Coke, he went off to see what they were up to. Five minutes passed, then another five.

Eventually Minh came walking back with a small owl in his hands! He had bought it from the boys because they were talking about killing it and he wanted to save it. Worried that they would just recapture it if he told them to set it free and leave it alone, he saw this as the only action he could take. Very admirable I know, but, I protested, what were we going to do with an owl? We couldn't release it here in case it was caught again. But we still had almost two hours' motorbike ride ahead of us and I hate touching birds. And what would we do with it in the city?

All my protests fell on deaf ears, however; Minh was a man with a mission to save this owl and bring it to Hanoi, and he went off to buy a woven basket used to carry ducks so we could transport it. Meanwhile, the drink stall lady and I wrapped the owl in the green-and-white striped towel we had brought with us and put it in a box while we waited for Minh to come back. He was gone for a long time and I was beginning to fear that I would be stranded here with an owl for company. He finally reappeared with a cage large enough to hold a whole family of owls and I knew that I wouldn't be able to hold it at the side of the motorbike all the way home while riding pillion. The drink stall lady and a gathering of locals were clearly enjoying this diversion. They probably rarely, if ever, got to see foreigners here or be involved in an owl rescue. When it was clear that the duck cage wouldn't work, the drink stall lady offered an old plastic shopping basket with handles that she had found, and we placed the tightly wrapped owl inside it and tied the handles together. Minh and I set off with the basket wedged between us, behind him and in front of me, so the owl was sheltered from the wind as we rode along.

Once we got a bit further down the road I broached the question of what Minh thought we were going to do with this owl.

It turned out he wanted me to keep it and look after it! I could just see myself trying to catch live mice for its supper and being kept awake with hooting all night. So I explored the possibility of him leaving it in the care of other friends who might have aviaries. But no luck. I was becoming increasingly alarmed at the prospect of being responsible for this poor little creature.

After about an hour on the road, the owl hadn't moved and I was becoming worried that we were carrying a dead owl back to Hanoi—which, of course, would have solved the feeding and care problem. I asked Minh to stop along the roadside so we could check it. At that stage, convinced by its deathly stillness, I was ready to move into my version of the Monty Python dead parrot skit ('This is an ex-owl, he's snuffed it, mate, he's pushing up the daisies') only there was no-one here to appreciate it. We carefully undid the basket handles and started to unwrap the towel when suddenly our owl came to life, struggling to get free. It had been playing possum! So we wrapped it up again, with its funny little round face poking out, and headed off, back down the road to Hanoi.

All the while I was racking my brain for ways to off-load this owl that would be acceptable to Minh. I had by this time managed to convince him that we couldn't feed it adequately or give it a good, safe environment to stay in. Suddenly I had an idea: the zoo, which we had to pass on our way home. By the time we reached the outskirts of the city the sun had set and the moon was starting to rise. Suddenly the owl came to life, struggling to escape into the night where it is at home. I was having a fit on the back of the motorbike because I didn't want to touch it, yet it was breaking free.

At last we reached the zoo but it was closed to visitors by that time. We found an unlocked entrance and eventually some night guards, who were drinking tea, but they were not interested in helping us, telling us to come back the next day. This was not an option as far as I was concerned. As we drove towards the exit, wondering what to do, we passed the bird enclosures and I suggested to Minh that we should see how strong the owl was, and if it wasn't hurt maybe we could just leave it in the zoo. It would have some company and access to food and water, and be safe from small boys trying to capture it—the perfect solution! So, on a nice grassy corner near some trees and water we set our owl free. Slowly it looked around, then after just a few minutes flew off and perched in a nearby tree. I was certainly relieved. We had done our good deed and, hopefully, the owl would now be safe, although maybe a little confused wondering how he came to be in a big city. And if he stayed around, I expect the zookeepers were also a bit confused the next day, wondering how they had acquired an extra owl.

Coming home and reverse culture shock

Once you have been seduced by Hanoi's charms it can be hard to escape. I had seen many foreigners leave—sometimes more than once—only to return again to Vietnam's bosom, dissatisfied with life anywhere else, unable to settle back home. For eight years I kept reinventing myself to adapt to whatever job opportunities arose that would keep me there; leaving had been unthinkable. Then, at Christmas time in 2001, after a phone call to my parents, I suddenly felt it was time to go home. I finally realised that, as wonderful as the experience had been, I was never going to be more than a foreigner in Vietnam, that there were things I would never understand about the place and the people, and meanwhile I was losing touch with friends and family back home.

During my years away I had returned to Australia several times for short visits, but always stayed with friends and relatives in a rather unreal holiday whirl. Suspecting I would need a period of adjustment after leaving Hanoi for good, I decided on a staged re-entry strategy to reduce the shock, akin to easing the bandaid off slowly. First, I stayed with friends in Bangkok for two weeks—not Hanoi, but still Asia. Then I flew to friends in Perth—Australia, but not quite Sydney. So it was in Perth that I heard my first 'G'day mate' in the airport arrival hall from Bermuda-socked customs agents, and saw my first Australian blue sky, vast and overwhelming after the grey of Asia.

The phenomenon of reverse culture shock is well known among returned expatriates, and it really is a shock, even when you are expecting it. Suddenly you find yourself incompetent, to varying degrees. I had lived in Australia for almost half a century, but now, after only eight years away, I didn't know how things worked any more. I looked like an Australian and sounded like an Australian, so that when I had to reveal my ignorance by asking how to perform simple tasks like banking, buying train or bus tickets or connecting a phone, it was assumed that I must be stupid. People would put on their kindergarten-teacher voice and speak slowly and loudly to me. I had become a foreigner in my own country. Even the Hong Kong-Chinese lady in my apartment building asked me if I was French or maybe Italian! Had I really changed so much?

Of course I recognised many changes in myself. It is impossible after living for eight years in a very different cultural environment not to be re-socialised. The bureaucratic and business environment in Vietnam forces everyone eventually (if you are to survive) to learn patience, to learn to go with the flow, to be inventive in solving problems and overcoming obstructions, to understand that 'no' doesn't necessarily mean 'no' and that nodding may not be agreement. Socially, I had learnt about charm, about getting on with life and making the best of things, about enjoying the moment. On the other hand, Australia had changed in the intervening years, too, and I found many of the preoccupations and attitudes of Australians now just as puzzling as those I encountered among Vietnamese when I arrived in Hanoi eight years earlier. Fitting back into Australian society was not going to be easy, especially when in Vietnam I was made to feel exotic, special, visible and in demand, whereas in Australia I was ordinary—dare I say invisible—and in no demand whatsoever!

The whiteness and variety of the cloud formations, the squinting brightness of the light and the flamboyant sunsets used to catch me by surprise during each trip back to Australia. And then I would forget again under the grey, inland, Hanoi skies, only to be enraptured once more on the next visit. This time was no different as I again experienced the vastness of Australia and the sprawl of Sydney, the blueness of the sky and the stunning beauty of the harbour and coastline. In fact, Sydney was looking better than ever after its sprucing up for the Olympic Games in 2000.

I found a perfect apartment to rent in Sydney; a left-hand turn out my front door and I was two hundred metres from Darling Harbour where something was always happening— jazz concerts, latin dance festivals, musical performances, exhibitions, street performers, fireworks displays—and where I could enjoy the ever-changing spectacle of the harbour in all its glory. A turn to the right out my front door and I was five minutes from Chinatown, where I could shuffle in the crowds on weekends, see lots of Asian faces and occasionally catch some smells and sounds of Hanoi.

Even though I had once lived on twenty-five acres of land on the outskirts of Sydney among the rolling hills of what used to be dairy cattle country, and later in a quiet coastal suburb on the South Coast of New South Wales, I now needed to live in the heart of the city. I needed that buzz of living in a metropolis, the crowds, the noises, the activity, the convenience. Going back to the places I had once lived to visit old neighbours, I wondered how they could stand the quietness and isolation, and I sympathised with those Vietnamese who came to Australia to study and were frightened and bored because there were not enough people around. On the pavements, no food stalls, street sellers, shoeshine boys, postcard sellers, hairdressers, welders, motorbike washers, or families relaxing, all the things that make up the atmosphere of Hanoi. No-one to pass your house selling fresh bread rolls for your breakfast, or naturally grown vegetables for your dinner that night, or a bunch of fresh flowers.

The population of Hanoi is not much greater than that of Sydney but it is much more efficiently packed together, Hanoi being one of the most densely populated cities in the world. While this means living space is cramped and almost no-one has a yard, it also means that you don't have to travel far to visit family and friends. No-one I knew in Hanoi lived more than a twenty-minute taxi or motorbike drive away, and Hanoians would complain if they had to travel more than a few kilometres to work. The idea of commuting one or two hours a day each way is unbelievable to Vietnamese, and I certainly found it difficult to readjust to the scale of Sydney and its sprawl.

I also felt lost without the usual collection of motorbike taxis sitting on the corner waiting to take me right to the door of wherever I wanted to go. I was too nervous to drive my car in the centre of the city or across the Sydney Harbour Bridge; I hadn't driven a car for eight years and anyway, parking was impossible. Even using public transport still required a fair amount of walking. All those times I had complained about *cyclo* drivers and motorbike drivers pestering me when I had wanted some exercise in Hanoi came back to me as I trudged wearily through the streets of Sydney. And I had forgotten about hills, Hanoi being almost completely flat, so the calf muscles in my legs were getting quite a workout.

I knew from holidays back home that it took a while to stop speaking slowly and carefully and enunciating each syllable. 'Why are you speaking to me like that?' my mother would complain, as I lapsed into my 'you-Tarzan-me-Jane' speak. Once I got into the swing of it, it was quite dazzling to be able to speak colloquially and carelessly, not to have to explain references, metaphors and the vernacular. I was reminded of the pleasure of public eavesdropping in the streets and cafés, although I did discover that I needed to brush up on the current 'in' phrases and jargon; these days in the city it seems that no-one is ever 'caught between a rock and a hard place' anymore, but everyone is working '24/7'.

I came back with no illusions that it would be easy fitting back into my old life. But I was ready to tackle these challenges, confident that the skills which had enabled me to survive all sorts of situations in exotic locations would see me through. Then I found that it was often the little things that caught me out.

Eggs, for one thing! I left the supermarket flustered on my first visit. Ten years ago in supermarkets there was a choice of small, medium and large eggs in a carton of twelve. Now I was being confronted with a wall of choices: free-range, dietary-enhanced, vegan, vegetarian and so on; 'politically correct' eggs in various sizes and quantities. But what had happened to normal, old-fashioned white eggs? I searched through the cartons of ordinary, supermarket medium-sized eggs and there was not a white egg to be found—they were all brown. I remember there might have been one or two brown eggs in a carton once. But all brown? Never. In Vietnam, eggs were still mainly white. These days they can be bought in cartons from the newer supermarkets in Hanoi, but most Vietnamese still buy them individually from street sellers carrying them in woven baskets hanging from a shoulder pole, choosing small or large, white or brown or speckled in-between, hen or duck eggs, one or one hundred. As for free-range, well, everything in Vietnam seems to be free-range. Kids and livestock! And the quality? The freshest and most golden yolks I have ever seen.

Fruit was a bit overwhelming, too. In or out of season you can buy any fruit you want in Australia. In Hanoi I had learnt to appreciate the pleasure of looking forward to the various seasons and the bounty each brought. Nothing whetted the appetite more than seeing an initial trickle of the season's first fruits turn into a cornucopia of delight at the height of the season, followed by a little sadness as supplies petered out at the season's end. The fruit sellers with their laden baskets provided a reminder of nature's cycles and that with loss comes a new compensation as another crop hits the streets. Better still, the fruit tasted the way I remembered fruit tasting as a child.

I certainly missed all the street food stalls in Hanoi, and I began to notice various foods that we lacked in Australia, like barbecued chicken's feet and duck's feet, pig's colon and uterus, all delicacies in Vietnam. What happened to all the chicken's feet, I wondered? All the chickens for sale in super-markets had their feet chopped off, so what did they do with them? If I could find them, could I make a killing by exporting them to Vietnam? Was someone already doing it?

My friend and ex-bookshop business partner, Minh, who arrived in Sydney soon after me to begin a university course, alerted me to a food supply I had never considered before: the city wildlife. The families of ducks living on the pond at Victoria Park next to Sydney University, the carp in Centennial Park, the seagulls at Bondi Beach, the pigeons, myna birds and sparrows on the city streets, even the pelicans at Wollongong Harbour, all came under his calculating eye. My horrified reac-tion to such a suggested feast reassured me that I hadn't become socialised to that particular pragmatic Vietnamese view of 'fair game', despite having been forced to experiment with some exotic dishes when living there. Now I understood why wildlife sightings of any kind were rare in Hanoi and why Vietnamese kept their pets locked up safely.

One of the things that all visitors to Vietnam comment on is the traffic and the terror that crossing a busy road instills in them. Now I was terrified of the traffic in Australia. I had to get used to cars driving on the opposite side of the road and found myself reciting an old childhood rhyme, 'look to the right, look to the left, look to the right again ...' to remind myself which way the traffic was coming from. I also had to learn to recalculate the speed of on-coming traffic, now mainly cars and not motorbikes and bicycles, before stepping off the kerb. Launching yourself out into the traffic without looking, as is done in Hanoi, would, I knew, result in death or at least strong abuse in Sydney. Drivers in Australia drove much faster and much more aggressively. On the other hand I was surprised to find that traffic stopped at red lights and pedestrian crossings. When traffic lights were first installed in Hanoi, nobody took any notice and police had to be placed on duty to make drivers conform, and they would chase after an offending motorbike or bicycle rider on foot and give them a whack with their baton.

I had never thought of myself as prudish, but I found the seemingly incessant bombardment of sexual images and messages extremely confronting when I first returned. It is alarming to note that as time passes I have become increasingly immune, and will no doubt stop noticing it at all soon. Of course Vietnam is not pure, despite the best efforts of the Ministry of Cultural Control, the police and their campaign against 'social evils', and Internet firewalls. The usual vices abound, but are not dished up as a daily diet of sexual scandals as reported in intimate detail on Western prime-time news, or in the newer raunchy and explicit television shows.

Another shock was the discovery of real estate pornography! After years of very modest living in Vietnam, though comfortable by Vietnamese standards, it was hard to cope with the luxury and extravagance I found here, and the focus on wealth. Most Australians have so many possessions and such large houses, and everyone, in Sydney at least, seemed obsessed with property and property values. Television was full of programs about house auctions, newspapers and magazines had coloured inserts showing the highest-priced homes on sale that week and glossy brochures of desirable residences for sale choked my letterbox daily. Everyone seemed to be getting their kicks from 'perving' on properties they couldn't afford. On the other hand, I noticed a huge increase in the amount of graffiti polluting our cities and in the number of homeless people living and begging on the streets—surely a clear and urgent signal that all is not well in our society.

Socially, I found I was no good at 'chit chat' any more. Local celebrities and stars were now largely unknown to me, the only Big Brother I had heard of was in Orwell's novel and even my knowledge of the Australian political scene was a bit fuzzy, the country's politics not being considered sufficiently important in world affairs to be reported in the *Vietnam News*. I knew nothing about the British royals any more, or Michael Jackson's latest escapade or almost anyone in Hollywood. Even the terrorist attack on the World Trade Center received only small coverage in Vietnam. I have noticed that slowly my brain is being recolonised by all this junk infotainment, not by design but by some sort of social osmosis. I am also being nudged back into conformity in all sorts of other ways—the way I dress, speak, act and even think, to some extent. And I don't think something is missing in a room any more if there isn't a bust or picture of Uncle Ho.

So many things regained, but also many things lost. I miss the sense of fun of the Vietnamese, their willingness to try anything, their cockiness and reluctance to admit they can't do something, their encouragement for any undertaking. I miss their devotion to learning and self-improvement. Every night, the entrances to the universities are gridlocked as part-time students flock to their classes after a day of work. IT training centres are crowded, with several students sharing a computer in the rush to pick up these new skills. English-language training classes are full, and with often no books and no decent teaching aids, learning takes place thanks to a relentless determination to succeed. In Australia, the reaction if I wanted to study something new, was usually, 'Why would you want to do that?' In Vietnam the response was usually, 'I can help you find a teacher.'

I miss the pride that people take in their intellectual, academic and artistic achievements, and their lack of embarrassment in expressing emotion. At a ceremony held at Vung Tau in the south of Vietnam, to celebrate the landing of the submarine telecommunications cable from Thailand, the secretary-general of the Directorate of Posts and Telecoms was moved to compose and recite a poem on the spot to mark the occasion. Representatives of the Western telecommunications companies attending were not sure what to make of this performance and shifted about uncomfortably. Once I went with an official party to visit the Telecommunications Training Centre in the backblocks of Da Nang, where we disturbed an absorbed director of the centre composing a poem in his lunch break, the muse having come upon him suddenly. I miss some of the flowery speech, the exaggerated compliments, the charm and politeness. Maybe it isn't always sincere, as some cynics maintain, but even so, it has to be preferable to crudeness or rudeness.

I miss the Vietnamese toughness, too—that ability to survive, to get on with whatever needs to be done, to suffer without complaint. I miss the lessons I learnt every day just by seeing the example of those around me. One of the most common reactions of visitors to Vietnam is the realisation of just how lucky most of us who live in Western, developed countries are. My own antidote to the occasional 'blues' was to stroll around the streets of Hanoi, people-watching. How could I possibly be justified in feeling miserable when these people were getting on with life as best they could, not a tear in sight?

The young postcard sellers and shoeshine boys, most of them orphans, some living on the streets and others given a roof over their heads by charity organisations, were always ready with a cheeky grin. I would watch them head off early each day with their armload of postcards or their wooden box of shoeshine materials for another long day of approaching tourists to eke out a living. Instead of the hangdog demeanour you might expect, they would be laughing together and cheerfully mucking about like kids everywhere. Old people who had suffering and hardship etched deeply on their faces were uncomplaining. When pressed, they might tell of great tragedy—the loss of so many family members, friends and neighbours, of hunger and suffering—but with great calmness and certainly no tears.

In Australia, the so-called lucky country, I was surprised to find that public crying seems to be on the increase, by sports stars, politicians, criminals, usually after losing a game or position or being found out in some wrongdoing. I attended the world premiere in Hanoi of a documentary film made about the My Lai massacre. This was a joint production between American and Vietnamese filmmakers and was sponsored by the Quakers. The film showed some graphic footage from this particularly ignoble incident of the Vietnam War, then moved to My Lai today and gave an update on those lives that had been so dramatically affected three decades before. The men from the US helicopter crew who attempted to stop the massacre and managed to save some of the Vietnamese villagers took part in the film. They talked about their role, their feelings and the impact the event had on their lives. They went back to the village for the filming and met some of the women they had saved that dreadful day. Although they were the heroes in the terrible story, they were still deeply afflicted with the collective guilt of their country and their countrymen. It was an emotional meeting and these big, tough American soldiers cried and cried while the women they had saved smiled and smiled and comforted them. These women who had lost all members of their families, who had suffered physical and emotional pain and were still struggling to survive a harsh existence in one of the poorest regions of one of the world's poorest countries, just got on with life and smiled.

Of course there are some things I don't miss. But they were all part of the package deal, a deal that was overwhelmingly positive, just like Australia's package. Gradually, I am learning how to be a Sydneysider again, although I still don't know what happened to all the letterboxes, or to all the service stations that used to be conveniently located on street corners. I am getting used to talking to machines and following push-button commands whenever I telephone; in fact, I am startled if a real person answers sometimes. I am even slowly getting used to the comparatively high costs of most goods and services. And to the size of people in Australia. Young people are becoming taller and I was shocked by the increase in the number of obese Australians, young and old. In Vietnam I matched the average height and weight of their population and it gave me quite a different view of life—literally. Not only could I see further and not feel hemmed in by crowds, but I began to understand the difference in the feeling of power. Looking eye-to-eye or even looking down on someone is a very different experience to almost always looking up. It can change your feeling of personal security, your attitude and demeanour.

As to my successful reintegration into Australian life? Maybe that isn't what I want just yet. I certainly appreciate more than ever the wonderful things Australia has to offer: the physical beauty and diversity, the educational and work opportunities, the health and legal systems, the rich social and cultural fabric, the fact that we have never had a war here or been subjugated by a foreign power—things I once took for granted. But I also want to maintain a critical edge and try to see our society with an outsider's eyes to make sure that we are protecting the good things and doing something about the bad things.

Living abroad can free you from many of the social constraints of your own culture. For me, living in Vietnam allowed me to indulge many of my fantasies, and so I sang and danced, I drummed and ping-ponged, rode motorbikes, owned a bookshop, consulted fortune tellers and ventured forth fearlessly, believing that my Vietnamese friends would keep me safe. Not only did they take good care of me, they were encouraging and supportive of anything I suggested, full of fun, ready to have a go, and they graciously shared their lives with me. I am no longer infatuated with Hanoi. It was the right time for me to leave. But it has been good this past year to write these stories and look back nostalgically as one would look back on the times spent with an old love and remember the most wonderful eight years of my life.

Dreams found and lost

The story of three generations of a
Vietnamese family living in Hanoi
in the 20th century

FAMILY TREE

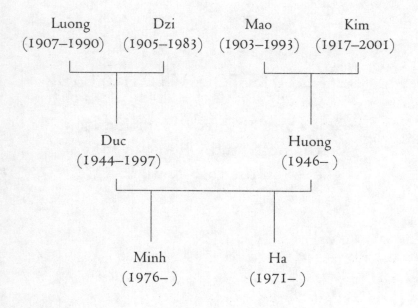

Luong (1907–1990)   Dzi (1905–1983)   Mao (1903–1993)   Kim (1917–2001)

Duc (1944–1997)   Huong (1946–)

Minh (1976–)   Ha (1971–)

Vietnamese culture has a long and glorious history dating back to the Bronze Age, but the 20th century has been a period of the most tumultuous and rapid social, political and economic changes in more than two millennia. The three generations of my friend and business partner Minh's family that span the 20th century cover the three distinct periods of change in that time—the French colonial era; the fight for independence from the French, the rise of communism and the war with the United States; and most recently, the more liberal policies of the 'open door' era and engagement with the West. His family offers, at a personal level, a glimpse into the impact of these broader forces on Vietnamese society. In these individual lives are reflected the hopes and dreams, the trials and tribulations of an entire society.

The Chinese were the first occupiers of Vietnam and they stayed more than one thousand years (*circa* 179BC–938AD), indelibly stamping the culture with a Chinese character. Once they finally wrested back control, the Vietnamese managed to hold on to their independence for almost another one thousand years until 1867, when South Vietnam became a French colony, and 1883 when Central and North Vietnam became French protectorates. After the occupation of France by Germany in World War II, the Japanese took advantage of the situation and occupied French Indochina in 1940. But with Japanese capitulation in August 1945, France attempted to re-establish its colonial power.

Finally ousted in 1954 following the famous battle at Dien Bien Phu, the French had only managed to stay a little over eighty years, but during that time they left a formidable legacy in every sphere of Vietnamese life. In Hanoi, the tree-lined boulevards, the lakes and parks and zoo, the large number of French colonial, Art Deco and Art Nouveau villas and houses, large and small, were all built under French rule. This vast building program was not only confined to the city of Hanoi. All over the country are reminders of French occupation, and one is left feeling that the French believed they would stay there forever, given the massive scale of construction.

But the French legacy is not confined to buildings and town planning; they have also strongly influenced Vietnamese language, food, the arts, education, style and fashion, and social customs. Today, most of the older Hanoians who were alive before 1945 speak French as their second language and as the weather changes, ushering in winter, the old men don their French berets and wrap their scarves French style inside their coats as they pedal ancient bicycles to sip coffee at sidewalk cafés. However, as in all stories of colonisation there is a darker legacy, one of subjugation of the local people and local culture, loss of power, exploitation and even brutality using the locals as slave labour. Nevertheless, many who worked with the French prospered, though such people remained a minority.

The thirty years after the end of World War II marked a period of intense national struggle for Vietnamese independence. First there was the struggle against the French and some skirmishes with the Chinese, followed by resistance to the United States from the early 1960s and finally with reunification of the country in 1975—the 'fall' of Saigon according to the West, but the 'liberation' of Saigon according to the North Vietnamese. Victory did not bring spoils to the victors though, just ten years of what many Vietnamese claim was greater hardship than the war years. During the war, at least there was a common outside enemy to fight against and justify the suffering. After, no-one had enough food and no family was immune to tragedy and hardship, the result of many years of war, US postwar embargo policies and the policies of the Vietnamese government and its experiment with communism.

When Uncle Ho went out into the world seeking support for an independent Vietnam in the 1940s, he first tried the United States and other Western countries, but the rebuffs pushed him into the arms of the then USSR. The influence of this relationship was not confined to political ideology and government administration, but is still evident in much of the architecture found in North Vietnam and in the generation of intellectuals who were educated in the USSR and who speak the languages of the Eastern European countries as their second language.

At the sixth Communist Party Congress at the end of 1986, a revolutionary step was taken which ushered in a new era in Vietnamese history. The period of *doi moi* or economic renovation (often referred to as the 'open door' policy) was introduced, and change came very rapidly. Within ten years, Vietnam was being touted in the business pages of the West as one of the new emerging Asian tigers and foreign investors were beating a path to Hanoi's door. Where the English language had once been banned, now it was becoming a prerequisite to obtain, and hold, a job. Students were no longer heading off to Eastern European countries to be trained as engineers and scientists; instead they wanted to study marketing and Western MBA courses.

The last decade of the 20th century saw incredible material changes in the society. Where once a family was lucky to have an old Chinese bicycle, now they were riding Honda Dream II motorbikes and even owning cars. Consumerism was rampant as everyone tried to outdo their neighbour with the latest television, stereo, washing machine or refrigerator. Time and money were also becoming available for leisure activities, shops were full of Western goods, pirated music and films, the young were adopting popular Western youth culture and wanting to study in Western countries. There was more openness to the world, the Internet became available and there were more and more foreigners coming as tourists and to work.

This then is a broad brush sketch of 20th century life in Hanoi, beginning with staid black-and-white images of French masters being pulled by Vietnamese *cyclo* drivers, followed by the heroic posters of communists building a new society and war propaganda, and ending up with psychedelic images of frenetic modern life, increasing traffic and a changing city skyline. To the outsider, this is an interesting and even exciting picture— a rich tapestry of a society undergoing rapid change. But it doesn't provide the human detail, the impact these changes had, not only on the material aspects of an individual's life but on their goals, hopes and dreams. The three generations of Minh's family spanning the 20th century provide some of that human detail, making the general personal, and giving some insights into the long-term effects these dramatic social upheavals had, and continue to have, on ordinary Vietnamese lives.

Minh and his sister were born in the 1970s and are part of that enormous demographic group in Vietnam, the post-Vietnam-War generation. Their parents' lives were forged by the struggle for independence, by the horror of war and by the ideology of communism, while their grandparents, who were born in the early years of the 20th century, lived through the height and then the end of the French colonial era. Each generation has been shaped by the times and has dreamed the dreams of those times. But some dreams turn into nightmares or are lost and forgotten by a new generation.

Mao was born in 1903 in a small village called Go, about twenty-five kilometres from Hanoi in Son Tay province (now called Ha Tay). Mao was a bright student and won a scholarship to attend a famous high school, then went on to study medicine at the Indochina Medical Institute in Le Thanh Ton Street in Hanoi. To become a fully qualified doctor at that time, graduates needed to complete another one or two years' study in France. Even though Mao's father was a non-commissioned officer in the French Army, and therefore paid a regular salary, the cost of studying in France for that length of time was beyond their means, and so after graduation Mao stayed on at the Medical Institute to work as a teaching assistant. During this period Mao enjoyed the good things of Hanoi life in the 1920s under the French. He had a reputation as a bit of a playboy and was known to visit geisha-like houses and opium dens of the day after being disappointed in his efforts to marry a Hanoi girl. Eventually, at what was then considered the late age of thirty-four, he settled down to married life with Kim.

Kim lived in Moc village on the outskirts of Hanoi, just a short tram trip from the centre. Her great-grandparents on one side had held a high position in the government administration in Hue, the old Vietnamese capital, and on the other side had been extremely rich, at one time owning more than ninety houses in Hanoi. Kim's father worked as an officer in the French administration. Kim's mother was given four houses by her well-off family when she married. She worried that her husband had many girlfriends and apparently used to read his mail, until thwarted by her husband when he instructed his correspondents to write in French, which she couldn't read. Kim's father died of liver disease in 1938 and her mother sadly died in poverty, having lost all her property and jewellery once the communists took control of Vietnam. Kim was not allowed to be educated past primary school, her mother saying that if she stayed on she would only write letters to boys and would be better off staying at home to learn cooking and other domestic crafts. However, her sister, who was only two years younger, was allowed to stay on at school and eventually became a teacher.

Kim's marriage to Mao, in 1937, was arranged by a matchmaker and while Mao was allowed to see his prospective bride, Kim was not allowed to see her husband-to-be until the wedding day. For their honeymoon they travelled by car with another couple to Saigon. However, not long after being married, Mao had a falling out with one of the Frenchmen at the Medical Institute. As a result, he lost his teaching post and had to complete a period of compulsory service as a medical worker, a lower level of local doctor, in the provincial regions of the North. First, Mao was sent to Bac Ha, a remote region around three hundred kilometres north-west of Hanoi, and in 1939 the couple's first child was born there.

Later, Mao and his young family moved to Phu Tho province, about one hundred kilometres from Hanoi, and then to Son Tay province, only about thirty kilometres from Hanoi. Once he had completed his period of compulsory service, the family returned to Hanoi and Mao opened a private medical practice in 1943. Mao and Kim were to have five children in all, the last when he was fifty-one and she was thirty-seven. Life was good for them under French rule. They lived in a nice house, owned a car and had a holiday house at Sam Son Beach. Kim sometimes went to the beauty salon in the exclusive Metropole Hotel, shopped at the best stores and owned lots of jewellery—not just gold, but pearls and diamonds which were much less common in Vietnam at the time. At one stage her grandparents owned a pet monkey that was notorious for stealing food and then trying to cover up the holes it left in the food. Her cousin taught her French and ballroom dancing. And she had tasted all the exotic foods of the time – wild cat, tiger, bear, bird's nest and even frogs and their eggs, said to be from the North Pole.

In 1946 when the French were trying to re-establish their colonial control, and fighting came to the streets of the capital, Mao and Kim fled Hanoi and their life changed forever soon after that. At first they still had money and could afford servants and a comfortable life in the countryside back in their home villages. Mao had earlier become interested in communism, and despite his privileged position in society under the French rule, believed in the communist ideals. Although he never joined the Communist Party (he was probably not able to as an intellectual at that time), he was known as a Patriot Doctor, working for the Vietminh with others such as the famous surgeon Ton That Tung, and he even visited China once on some communist business. The struggle between the Vietminh and the French continued and Kim eventually returned to Hanoi in 1949. When she tried to recover all her jewellery, which had been buried for safe keeping, she found most of it had been stolen, so was left with little money. With the help of relatives, she subsequently opened a gold shop in Hang Bac Street to earn a living.

By 1954 when the French finally left North Vietnam, Mao and Kim and their families had lost most of their assets and wealth. To avoid public criticism they had to conceal the fact that they owned some land at Hai Duong which they rented to a rice farmer. It was no longer legal to have gold, so they now had no business and had lost everything. In 1957 they moved to the northern port city of Hai Phong, where Mao became director of the ophthalmic department at Viet Tiep hospital. He remained there until his retirement in 1970 and the family returned to Hanoi. On their return, they stayed in Kim's sister's house, sharing with seven people—a tight squeeze where there was not the luxury of separate bedrooms, just enough space for beds.

In the later years of his life, Mao questioned whether he had been right to follow the communists. He regretted the hardship his wife had suffered as a result and was disappointed with his life after its early promise. However, on his death in 1993 at age ninety, Mao's family was surprised by the number of people from his old village who remembered him and came to Hanoi to pay their respects at his funeral.

Before she died of breast cancer in 2001, at the end of a long life of mixed fortune, Kim told her grandson, Minh, that she had tasted the best of luxury and the worst of poverty. Even with the benefit of hindsight, it is hard to know what the best course of action would have been. Kim's uncle, fearing the worst for Vietnam due to the rise of communism, had sent his three children off to different corners of the world before 1954. One went to the United Kingdom (where he still lives), one to France, and the other to Saigon and then, after 1975, to the United States. After 1954, Kim's uncle ended up being arrested and jailed for being a landowner. He hanged himself in jail, leaving his wife to struggle in poverty until the 1980s when her sons living overseas could finally send her some money for support.

Huong, the fourth child of Mao and Kim, was born in January 1946 not long before the family left Hanoi to escape the conflict. Huong returned to Hanoi with them in 1949, but when her parents and siblings later went to Hai Phong, she stayed on in Hanoi and lived with her grandmother. She attended the nearby public school and high school, and it was in high school that Huong met her future husband, Duc. Her early childhood was spent in the area known as Hanoi's ancient thirty-six streets, also known as the old quarter, a bustling centre of commerce, and she had lots of relatives to visit nearby. On completing high school, Huong attended the same medical school as her father, by now called the Hanoi Medical School following the departure of the French. After two years of study there, she was transferred to the Army Medical Institute 103 in Ha Dong to complete her training during the war years. In her last year of university, Huong joined the army and after graduation stayed on at the Army Medical Institute as a teacher.

In those days, university students and intellectuals were required by the communist government to work in the fields and mix with the peasants, and high school students were required to undertake social tasks such as working through the night helping prepare Hanoi's Da Binh Square for National Day celebrations. One day, when Huong was unwell and her future husband helped to take her to work in the fields, she was criticised and told she was behaving like a member of the old landowner class who expected to be looked after. At times, during Operation Rolling Thunder, when the United States bombarded the North for three-and-a-half years from March 1965 to October 1968, the universities and hospitals had to evacuate Hanoi and on one of these occasions Huong recalls watching an emergency appendix operation being performed in a pagoda, with no electricity and no anaesthetic. The patient was screaming with pain and had to be tied down, and moths attracted to the lantern light were falling into the wound. In 1969, Huong was married to Duc, her old high school friend and neighbour.

Duc was born in 1944, his parents' seventh and last child and his mother's favourite. His father, Luong, the son of the head official of his village, became a school teacher and was twenty-five years old when he married Dzi, who was two years older than him—an unusual situation in Vietnam. Dzi's father had been an Army officer in one of the mountainous regions of the North, but he died early, leaving Dzi as the eldest child to help look after and support her siblings by working as a material seller.

Luong and Dzi's first child, who was born in 1931 and attended university in China, was one of the founders of the Hanoi University of Technology (HUT). The youngest son, Duc studied electrical engineering at HUT from 1962 to 1966, and after graduation went to work at the Nam Dinh power station, eighty kilometres from Hanoi, travelling back to Hanoi each weekend to see his then girlfriend, Huong. In 1970 he transferred back to the HUT in Hanoi and became a teacher there for the rest of his life. But even after marriage, Duc and Huong were not destined to always be together, since schools and universities still had to evacuate Hanoi at various times, and as they both worked for different institutions they were sent to different locations, often only meeting each other on weekends. During the 1972 US attacks on Hanoi, Huong had to evacuate the city and take her small daughter—Ha, born in 1971—in a wire basket attached to her bicycle to her father's village of Go. After the Paris Agreement, signed in January 1973, the family returned to Hanoi.

Duc's parents had also evacuated Hanoi, leaving their house for soldiers to live in. Civilians who stayed in Hanoi during the war were given warnings through the city's public speaker system to go to bomb shelters whenever enemy planes were spotted on their way. The Americans bombed the Long Bien Bridge, Bach Mai Hospital, Hanoi railway station and even sent a rocket into a house in Hue Street not far from Duc's parents' house. Between bombing raids, the city was quiet and the streets almost empty. Anti-US posters were everywhere, demanding that Nixon would have to pay back the blood he had taken. Villagers would be rewarded if they captured any of the enemy and there was often fierce competition between neighbouring villages. An American plane was shot down over Ngoc Ha flower village and its almost submerged wreckage can still be seen, sticking out of a small pond. A plaque marks the place another plane was shot down and its pilot captured near West Lake.

Life was hard during the war, but just as hard for many years after. There were frequent power cuts and even when there was power available it was very weak and lighting was usually dim. The streets were still quiet, as people had nowhere to go. Everyone wore plastic sandals and peasant-style clothes. School books were scarce and expensive and children often stitched brown paper sheets together to make notebooks. Food was in short supply and family connections with anyone who worked in food production were important. The normal food coupons provided just 100g of meat per month, which was usually taken as fat to use for cooking, and 13kg of rice per month, usually poor quality and often adulterated with small stones. Huong received a ration of 21kg of rice per month because of her army position. The A-grade stamps which could be used in the special international shops near Hoan Kiem Lake were only available to high-ranking officials and government ministers.

Ordinary people became skilled at stretching food. Children were sent to collect tiny crabs living in ponds. Eggs, when available, were fried and cut in half to stretch to make two meals. If a family was lucky enough to somehow find a chicken to eat, it did so behind closed doors and windows, making sure to bury the bones and feathers far away to avoid any questions from jealous neighbours. To supplement his small university salary, Duc repaired television sets on the side, and once in 1975 he took a boat to Saigon to buy goods such as second-hand fridges, televisions, even a Lambretta motor scooter, and brought them back to Hanoi to trade.

Then in 1978, when his daughter was seven and his son only two, Duc applied for a scholarship to study for his doctorate in Moscow, where he stayed for five years until 1983. A few months before he left for Moscow, Duc and his wife and two small children moved to Ha Dong to a small fourth-floor apartment with a shared kitchen and bathroom. Even though it was only twelve kilometres from the centre of Hanoi, at that time it was considered the countryside, with rice fields and little else. His wife and children stayed there until 1981; by this time Minh was attending kindergarten and his sister was at primary school. But three years of living in the countryside without her husband was enough for Huong, so she decided to apply to study her PhD at the medical university as a way of moving back to Hanoi to live in her aunt's house.

Under the Vietnamese system, Huong would still receive her normal doctor's pay while studying, and when possible, her husband would send goods from the USSR for her to sell to supplement her meagre income. Once, Duc sent his daughter a doll that cried and opened and closed its eyes, and his son a train set and truck, a gift so luxurious and exotic at that time that Minh couldn't let go of it and was too excited to sleep. In 1981, Duc wanted to come back to Hanoi for a holiday to see his family, but he was warned by his family not to do this. When his older brother, who had been to Moscow in the 1970s to study his PhD, came back to Vietnam for a holiday he wasn't allowed to return to complete his studies because it was claimed he had been critical of communism, even though he was a member of the party. When Vietnamese were allowed to travel overseas they were always put in groups of three, and they had to keep records and report on each other. However, Duc was making the most of his time in Moscow and was enjoying himself. He had grown his hair long (although he cut it short before returning home), played guitar, went camping with Russian friends, all of which was recorded and reported and which could potentially cause trouble for him.

When Duc finally returned to Hanoi in 1983, his children were twelve and seven years old and hardly knew him. Young Minh couldn't call him father at first, calling him uncle instead. And it was just as hard for Duc to adjust after five years away living a free and single life in a very different culture. To celebrate his return, Duc took his wife out rowing on West Lake, but for the first few months after his return he mainly stayed at home and lay in the sun or took photos and developed them using a kit he had brought back with him. After he went back to the university to take up his teaching position again, he sometimes talked about escaping like 'boat people', or moving south to Ho Chi Minh City where it was believed that life was better—but this remained only talk. In 1988, Duc applied for the title of professor at his university, but he was not successful because he was not a member of the Communist Party.

Huong finished her PhD in 1987 and in 1988 she was required to join the Party in order to keep her job, since she had now reached the level of army major. Then in 1990, Duc's father, Luong, decided to sell the house where Duc and his family were now living with the old man (Duc's mother had died in 1983, just before her son returned from Moscow). The extended family decided to buy a house in Khuong Thuong village near Hanoi where they would have enough land for a garden, but just before they moved in, the old man Luong died.

The sale of the house went ahead. With some of the proceeds of the sale, Duc bought a colour television and a VCR, a considerable luxury at that time costing the equivalent of almost US$400 each. This was the family's first colour television; in the mid-1980s they had had a second-hand black-and-white television bought from Saigon, there being no new televisions for sale in Hanoi at that time. Not that there was much to watch; only one channel operated for about three hours each day showing news, traditional music, an occasional film from Eastern Europe with Vietnamese dubbing and sometimes children's shows. Minh remembers seeing a Disney show with Donald Duck and the Chipmunks when he was about eleven years old, and all the children at that time enjoyed Russian cartoons about a rabbit and wolf and another show about a character called Micah who had a magic ring.

With the advent of the 'open door' era, the family fortunes began to improve. Life was more stable, food was available and Duc was able to earn extra money working for various companies outside the university, designing hydroelectric machines and paper-making equipment. He also did a little trading, and even travelled back to Russia a few times on business. Then in 1997 he was invited to present a paper at a conference in

Barcelona and decided to extend this trip to visit his daughter, Ha, who was now living in France, and then call on old friends in Russia before heading back to Hanoi. He was excited at the prospect of visiting capitalist countries and seeing his daughter. However, the trip was to have a tragic end.

After visiting Ha in France, Duc flew to Moscow. On arrival at Moscow airport, he took the train only a short distance to where his friend lived. He carried his luggage from the train to the apartment block, rang the apartment number and was let inside the building by his friend's daughter, but he never made it to the apartment. Between the lift and the apartment, he was stabbed in the neck and left to die. Even today, the motive for the murder is not clear. Not all his money was stolen—US$300 was found on him. So whether he was a random victim in a country where lawlessness was becoming the norm, or whether he was mistaken for someone else will never be known. His ashes were brought back to Hanoi by a nephew who was working in Moscow at the time, back to a wife and son whose life had only recently begun to get a little easier, but who would now have to struggle alone with new challenges.

Ha, Huong and Duc's daughter, was born in 1971, a tiny baby who even as an adult never reached more than 153cm and 42kg. She was a bright student and was selected to study at the prestigious Hanoi–Amsterdam high school in Hanoi, before going on to study computer science at the Hanoi University of Technology. At home, there was often talk about her studying overseas and marrying a foreigner as a means to a secure future and thus happiness.

Ha initially hoped to study in an Eastern European country, but she was unsuccessful in winning a scholarship. However, at that time Vietnam was beginning to open up to the West more than ever before and so she began to look at the possibility of studying in a Western country. She had studied some English at school but there were few good English-language schools in Hanoi at that time, so she turned to the Alliance Française and began to study French seriously. In 1994 she won a scholarship and set off to France to study for her Masters degree in Computer Science, and by 1996 she had not only graduated but had married a French–Madagascan classmate and stayed in France, fulfilling the family dream.

Minh, her younger brother, also followed the family tradition of studying at the Hanoi University of Technology. A serious bout of hepatitis and the death of his father interrupted his university studies for a while, but eventually he graduated with the degree of Bachelor of Enterprise Administration in 2001. He too had been infected by family talk of studying overseas. Even though his father was unimpressed with the USSR after his five-year stay there, he liked the people and would sometimes talk about Minh marrying his Russian friend's daughter. But Minh was also influenced by the steadily increasing flow of foreigners from the West coming to Hanoi and the popular images of the good life to be had there. While helping me set up a bookshop in Hanoi in 2001, he began to seriously study English and in 2002 he set off for Australia to study, first computer network management at TAFE, then a postgraduate diploma in translation and interpreting. Another family member seemed on the way to fulfilling the family dream. But was the dream, perhaps, flawed?

The lives of Minh's grandparents had initially been privileged and comfortable, albeit under foreign rule, and later, to varying degrees, they embraced the ideals of communism until that dream turned sour. When they lost their wealth and privilege, they had at least a belief in communism to turn to, but when that failed them, what was left for them to believe in and hope for?

Minh's parents were indoctrinated at school and university with nationalistic and communistic zeal and talked of building a new society together as they set out on their married life. But they faced many hardships and disappointments. Minh's father, Duc, had believed in the communist ideals as a young man; he even cried when Uncle Ho died. But after 1975 Duc began to have his doubts, and after living in Russia for five years he understood that the communist experiment had not worked there either. He saw the poverty and hardship in the Russian countryside and the breakdown of infrastructure there while a facade of modernity was maintained in Moscow to give the illusion of success to the rest of the world. To provide for his family he had to resort to capitalist means. Given his disenchantment, it is little wonder, therefore, that the idea of going to the West was planted so strongly in his children. Here was a new dream for a new generation. And they had other role models: Vietnamese families—at least those with education and means—had a tradition of hedging their bets, even back in the days before 1954 as communism rose and the future for Vietnam was looking uncertain, by sending their children to various Eastern and Western countries to live, work and study.

So what about the current generation, the inheritors of those new dreams born out of disappointment and frustration? Ha, now a French citizen, is living in France with her husband and two small daughters. When she had her second baby, her mother Huong, went to France to stay with her for a couple of months. Although thrilled to see her daughter and grandchildren, Huong knew that even if she was permitted to live in France, she couldn't survive there for very long. At her age, with no French language skills, no friends and no work, she would have a very small life in Paris compared to her life and status in Hanoi. On the other hand, when Ha, now a wife and mother, returned to Hanoi for a visit, she found a very different city to the one she had left as a young university student—a city which now offered many opportunities to the young and educated. In Hanoi she saw that these days she could retain a comparable or even higher living standard to the one she had in France, and she would be within her own culture surrounded by family and friends. Only now she had a husband to consider; a husband who would be isolated by language and culture if they moved to live in Vietnam. And she had two daughters—French daughters—whose future she must consider. Ha is caught between two worlds that she cannot integrate—her Vietnamese family can't be part of her life in France and her French family can't make a life in Vietnam. Would she have been better off holding on to the dream her parents once shared of building a new society in Vietnam?

Her young brother Minh is studying in Australia in the hope of obtaining permanent residency and ultimately Australian citizenship. Yet as his studies draw to an end, he is starting to question whether Australia is what he really wants. Unfortunately, in order to gain the experience to judge, he is already set on that pathway with not much hope of turning back now that the family money has been spent to give him his chance. So, like his sister, he too wonders if he could have been completely satisfied staying in Hanoi. What about the dream they imagined and their parents and grandparents imagined for them? Have they achieved material satisfaction at the expense of spiritual and emotional needs which are tied so closely to their home country? Can they ever overcome their homesickness for Hanoi and their separation from family and friends, and find a feeling of belonging and a way of life that is totally satisfying in a foreign country? Was the dream flawed in not recognising this, just as the dreams of earlier generations were flawed?

Life in Hanoi changed so rapidly in the last few years of the 20th century. Vietnamese who have lived overseas are beginning to come back. Government policies are becoming increasingly libe-ral as they try to find a way between communism and capitalism, between East and West, between traditional and modern ways. But there is still a long way to go as the government takes two steps forward and one step back, perhaps fearing they have opened the door a bit too far. Vietnamese are pragmatists and so continue to hedge their bets. But it seems that once a Hanoian, always a Hanoian, whether they are living in New York, Paris or Sydney. So what will be the dream of the next generation, the children of Ha and Minh? To assimilate into the Western society adopted by their parents. To water down the Vietnamese genes through intermarriage? Or to return to Hanoi and build the new society their great-grandparents once dreamed of? Where will they feel they belong?

Chronology

1862   Emperor Tu Duc surrenders South Vietnam to the French; the colony of Cochin-China is born.

1883   Central and North Vietnam become the French Protectorates of Annam and Tonkin.

1930   Ho Chi Minh forms Indochinese Communist Party.

1940   September: Japanese occupy Indochina following Germany's occupation of France; French retain figurehead authority only.

1945   August: Japanese capitulation. France attempts to re-establish its colonial power in Indochina.

1945   September: Ho Chi Minh becomes president, with Hanoi as capital. He declares independence for Vietnam from France and negotiates with France.

1946   France begins rebuilding colonial administration and Vietminh increase attacks against French forces in North and South.

1953   November: French install garrison at Dien Bien Phu, intended to control border region between North Vietnam and North Laos.

1954   French are defeated in defining battle at Dien Bien Phu and subsequently surrender. Vietnam is then divided into communist North, controlled by Ho Chi Minh, and capitalist, US-supported South, controlled first by Bao Dai then by Ngo Dinh Diem. National elections to unify country are expected to be held after two years, but never eventuate.

1961   US President Kennedy sends in first military ' advisers'.

1962   Eleven thousand US troops sent to South Vietnam.

1963   South Vietnamese President Diem is overthrown and killed.

1964   August: Tonkin Gulf incident where North Vietnamese forces attack a US destroyer.

1965   Operation Rolling Thunder begins in March; ordered by US President Johnson, the bombardment of North Vietnam continues for 3 ½ years until October 1968. During this time, 1 million tons of bombs are dropped on Vietnam.

1968   January: Tet offensive. A surprise attack by communist forces on the South Vietnamese and US forces.

1969   Negotiations begin in Paris. Ho Chi Minh dies. Number of US troops in country reaches 543,000.

1972   North Vietnam invades South Vietnam. More intensive US bombing of North.

1973   January: Cease-fire signed in Paris.

1973   March: Last US troops leave South Vietnam.

1975   April: North occupies Saigon and country is reunified. War ends.

1975   Saigon changes its name to Ho Chi Minh City.

1978   Vietnam invades Cambodia over border disputes. China attacks Vietnam.

1986   Sixth Vietnamese National Party Congress announces plan for economic renovation, known as *doi moi*.

1990   EC (now EU) establishes official diplomatic relations with Vietnam. Vietnam reaches peace agreement with Cambodia and restores diplomatic relations with China.

1994   United States removes trade embargo.

About the author

Originally trained in pharmacy, Pam Scott later undertook further studies as she raised her two sons, finally graduating with a PhD in science and technology policy in 1986. She then worked as an academic at Wollongong University before moving to the commercial arm of the university to work at the Centre for Information Technology Research in 1992. She first visited Vietnam in late 1993 and moved there to live in early 1994. She came home to Australia in 2002 for eighteen months before returning to Vietnam in September 2003 for a short-term consultancy.